FRONTLINE LEADER
COACHING

The Language of Empowerment

Blessing Moyo

Copyright © 2025

All rights are reserved, and no part of this publication may be reproduced, distributed, or transmitted in any manner, whether through photocopying, recording, or any other electronic or mechanical methods, without the explicit prior written permission of the publisher. This restriction applies to any form or means of reproduction or distribution.

Exceptions to this rule include brief quotations that may be incorporated into critical reviews, as well as certain other non-commercial uses that are allowed by copyright law. Any such usage must adhere to the specified conditions and permissions outlined by the copyright holder.

ISBN: [978-0-9756428-0-1]

© 2025 Blessing Moyo

Dedication

To all who walk with me,
*I am deeply grateful to each of you for the
profound impact you've had on my life.
My Clan:
Urilile, Riah, Prisca, Nams, NomaQ, Sisa, Thamu,
Mdu, CP ,Lisang (PK),Cee and Destyni—your love and
unwavering presence ground me.
You are my anchor and my joy.*

*Lalu: Kea leboga – Kumbudzi, Thobela, Malaba,
Mkhubazi, Gumbu, Ncube.
Bagudu ba Njelele.
Dombo lisingapotelekwe likapotelekwa kukama
Mivumbi!*

Robati: Dewa, Sayi, Vumabalanda, Mageza ngochago,
Amageza amahle aza wodwa,
Moyo omnyama Sayi.
Yithi laba esigeza ngochago abanye begeza
ngamanzi.
Iqhawe lasendulo elahlalisa uMzilikazi
ebukhosini bakhe.
Khumbuza... Mdlahlezi.

To all those who walked before me
known and unknown—I honour you.
My words are not new, they are echoes before

me and dreams held in the breath.
I do not create — I remember.
I do not perform — I awaken.
I am the river that remembers its source.

Acknowledgments

I would like to extend my heartfelt gratitude to those who have profoundly impacted my professional journey. Your mentorship, support, and guidance have been invaluable in shaping who I am today as a Leadership Coach.

Tracy Cousins, your trust and encouragement have empowered me to reach new heights and strive for excellence. It was my first realisation to dare to dream that I could be more than what I was.

Angela Winterbourne, your belief in my worth and value was transformative. You allowed me the space to discover my true potential, and your support was a cornerstone of my professional growth.

Iain Hegarty, your mastery in managing upwards has been an art form that I strive to emulate. Your lessons on navigating organisational dynamics with grace and effectiveness have been invaluable.

Morgan Jones, your heart and empathy for people have been a constant source of inspiration. Your ability to connect with others on a profound level has taught me the true essence of compassionate leadership and ubuntu.

Kevin Russell, you have an incredible gift for seeing past the exterior and understanding the true nature of others. Your perceptive insights have helped me appreciate the depth and potential in everyone I encounter.

Jamie McCormick, thank you for expanding my horizons and enhancing my approach to problem-solving. Your ability to curate complex strategies has been instrumental in my development.

Paul Fox, your unwavering belief in my abilities and your encouragement to back myself have been pivotal. You showed me how to trust my natural insight-gathering abilities, and for that, I am deeply grateful.

How to Use This Book

"The Language of Empowerment: Frontline Leader Coaching."

Welcome to a transformative journey in leadership. This book is your indispensable guide as a new leader aiming to build and lead high-performing teams. It is packed with straightforward, practical advice for handling the real-world challenges of frontline leadership.

Imagine this book as your personal coach. Beyond theory, it is filled with vivid examples and analogies that show you exactly how to apply these ideas to your team. Picture yourself as a newly promoted team leader, eager to enhance your department's performance. This guide will walk you through each step, offering not just considerations but actionable recommendations. You'll find practical tips on changing behaviours and attitudes within your team, fostering an environment where everyone is united in their efforts.

What sets this book apart is its emphasis on real-life application. Think of it as a roadmap for your leadership journey—one that blends theoretical concepts with practical steps. This approach ensures you can implement these lessons in your unique situation and see tangible results. Whether you are leading a team for the first time or seeking to refine your skills, this book provides the essential tools for success.

This book emphasises continuous learning and self-improvement, encouraging you to reflect on your experiences and observe team dynamics. Connecting theoretical concepts with real-life scenarios makes the content engaging and easier to grasp.

By adopting the strategies in this guide, you'll enhance your leadership capabilities and inspire your team to reach their fullest potential. Dedication to self-improvement and leading by example are championed here, fostering lasting success and establishing you as an exemplary leader.

The Genesis of This Book

I didn't set out to write a book.
I set out to respond to a pull.

Over the years, I've coached dozens of frontline leaders—on mine sites, in plants, on the floor, in offices often stepping into roles where expectations were high, but guidance was minimal. And time after time, when my working contract came to an end, I'd hear the same thing:

"Can you leave us something?"
Something solid. Something real.
Something we can lean on when you're not here.

This book is my response to that ask. It's a collection of the thinking, tools, and coaching approaches I've used to help leaders shift—not just in what they *do*, but in how they *see*. It's built from years of watching people step into leadership roles without a guide—expected to navigate complex people challenges with nothing but their technical expertise and a good attitude.

Like Anthony.

He was a brilliant technician. He knew the plant inside out, diagnosed faults fast, and ran a clean shift. But the moment he became a supervisor, the game changed. The problems weren't mechanical anymore. They were behavioural, emotional, relational. And those don't come with step-by-step fault codes.

At first, Anthony tried to lead like he fixed machines: find the problem, apply the fix, move on. But it didn't work. His team didn't shift. That's when he started looking inward—asking better questions, slowing down, learning to coach instead of correct. That shift—from knowing to growing—is what this book is about.

Not everyone gets a coach.
Not every company has a system for building leadership habits.
So think of this as the next best thing.

Case Study:

The Gold Lotto Test

The Gold Lotto Test is a powerful thought experiment designed to help leaders evaluate the effectiveness of their teams. Imagine a scenario where a high-performance team wins the lottery and resigns. The next day, a new team must step in and seamlessly continue the work.

This test highlights the importance of reproducibility and repeatability in processes, which are crucial for a team's ability to produce consistent, predictable, and reliable results. These factors are vital for an organisation's long-term sustainability and its ability to maintain intellectual property and viability.

To pass the Gold Lotto Test, a team must have systems and processes so well-designed that new members can replicate past results without disruption. That means:

- **Reproducibility**: Achieving the same results when a process is executed by different people, using different tools, or at different times. This requires controlling inputs, standardising processes, and training team members to follow established methods.

- **Repeatability**: Achieving consistent results when the same person runs the process multiple times under the same conditions. This depends on well-documented procedures, properly calibrated equipment, and strong adherence to standard operating protocols.

Common Challenges in Achieving Reproducibility and Repeatability

Teams often struggle with reproducibility and repeatability due to several common issues:

1. **Lack of Standardisation:** Without standardised procedures, different team members may perform tasks in varying ways, leading to inconsistent results.
2. **Resistance to Documentation:** Teams may resist thorough documentation, viewing it as time-consuming or unnecessary, which can hinder knowledge transfer and process consistency.
3. **Inadequate Calibration and Maintenance:** Equipment that is not properly calibrated or maintained can produce unreliable results, undermining the repeatability of processes.

Consider a healthcare team in a busy hospital. This team is responsible for managing patient intake, treatment plans, and discharge procedures. Now, imagine the entire healthcare team wins the lottery and resigns. A new team must step in the very next day and seamlessly continue the patient care processes left behind by the previous team.

To pass the Gold Lotto Test, the healthcare processes must be meticulously documented, with clear treatment protocols, patient records, and standardised procedures for patient care. Proper training and orientation for new team members ensure that patient care remains consistent and reliable, even in the face of sudden personnel changes.

By focusing on robust processes and effective knowledge transfer within a team, team leaders can develop a high-performance team prepared to handle any challenge.

The Gold Lotto Test underscores the value of solid processes and seamless knowledge sharing within a team, ensuring the team's resilience and adaptability in the face of change, ultimately contributing to the overall success of the organisation.

Actionable Steps

As you reflect on whether your team would pass this test, consider the following actionable steps:

1. **Evaluate your team's processes:** Are your workflows clearly documented, standardised, and repeatable by others without guidance?
2. **Analyse knowledge sharing and documentation:** Is critical information stored in a way that's easily accessible and transferable to new team members?
3. **Review training and development:** Do new hires receive consistent, comprehensive training that prepares them to maintain performance immediately?
4. **Monitor team dynamics:** Look for behavioural cues—such as collaboration, adaptability, and problem-solving—that indicate your team can maintain performance under pressure.

Reproducibility and repeatability are vital for maintaining quality in high-turnover environments. In healthcare, for example, consistent documentation and standardised practices have helped ensure stable patient outcomes even during staff transitions.

These standardised processes ensure that new healthcare teams can maintain high levels of care and patient satisfaction even during significant personnel changes.

By reflecting on these aspects, you can identify areas of improvement and take actionable steps towards building a team that not only passes the Gold Lotto Test but also thrives in the face of change. This self-reflection and proactive approach to team development will contribute to the long-term success of your organisation, fostering a culture of adaptability, resilience, and high performance.

Remember, the Gold Lotto Test is not just a theoretical concept but a practical tool to help you assess and improve your team's readiness for change and ability to maintain high performance under any circumstances.

Table of Contents

Part 1: Coaching Is Leadership 13
    Chapter 1: The Real Work on the Frontline 15
    Chapter 2: The Shift from Command to Capability 22
    Chapter 3: The Hidden Cost of Not Leading 30
    Chapter 4: Leadership Behaviours That Stick 35

Part 2: Build Your Toolkit 45
    Chapter 5: Leading with Insight Builds Capability 47
    Chapter 6: Growth That Happens on the Job 53
    Chapter 7: Bringing Standards to Life 60
    Chapter 8: Development Is a Team Sport 74

Part 3: Design What Good Looks Like 89
    Chapter 9: A Playbook That Actually Works 91
    Chapter 10: Next-Level Leadership Conversations 104
    Chapter 11: When Feedback Becomes a System 120
    Chapter 12: Leader Standard Work Is Core Work 134

Part 4: When Growth Outlives You 147
    Chapter 13: The Signals of Real Progress 149
    Chapter 14: When Habits Turn Into Culture 161
    Chapter 15: The Spiral of Legacy 172

References 179

PART 1:

COACHING IS LEADERSHIP

Why the real work of leadership is building belief, not control

Chapter 1:

The Real Work on the Frontline

Navigating inconsistent performance in frontline teams is like decoding a shifting code. Picture a team that shines one month and struggles the next. This inconsistency isn't just a fluctuation in numbers; it's a signal pointing to deeper, underlying issues within the system. Frontline workers, whether they are factory operators or retail associates, face numerous challenges that contribute to this variability.

These challenges can range from receiving unclear instructions, which can be as confusing as a complex puzzle, to adapting to rapidly changing procedures, akin to trying to hit a moving target. Additionally, the struggle with inadequate tools can leave these workers feeling as if they are expected to build a house without a hammer and nails.

Inconsistent performance can send shockwaves throughout an organisation. A missed deadline triggers project delays, which leads to customer dissatisfaction—and, over time, this can damage the organisation's reputation, a hard-earned and fragile asset. For frontline workers, inconsistency often creates an environment of confusion and instability. It can feel like navigating a maze without a map—disorienting and draining morale. For leaders, addressing this challenge is critical, as it influences not just individual performance but the overall health and resilience of the organisation.

For new leaders especially, striking a balance between the 'hard' aspects of work (like systems and processes) and the 'soft' aspects (such as team culture and morale) is a complex challenge. It's like an acrobat performing a balancing act, where too much focus on one aspect can cause the other to falter. This challenge is about understanding the interplay between these aspects and how they contribute to the team's overall performance.

For the frontline perspective, technical changes can often feel disconnected from the reality of daily work. A new inventory system might look impressive on paper but fail to fit their workflow or feel intuitive. This disconnect breeds frustration and resistance. Effective leadership requires recognising that what works strategically must be translated into something practical and workable on the ground.

Change, especially in a frontline setting, can be an unsettling, if not turbulent experience for workers. They often find themselves directly impacted by new systems and processes yet may not fully grasp the reasons behind these changes. Being asked to change a well-practiced routine without understanding the benefits or seeing the bigger picture can be disorienting. The challenge here is the potential resistance and confusion that can arise from such changes. Leaders must navigate these waters carefully, understanding that change is not just a process but an experience for those involved.

The challenge of aligning the frontline workforce with organisational changes is a complex task. It goes beyond merely announcing new processes or systems. It's about helping the workforce understand and adapt to these changes. This challenge involves turning a new vision into practical terms that the frontline team can easily understand. It involves acknowledging their concerns and integrating their feedback and experiences into the change process.

A common challenge for leaders is the potential gap between their perception and the frontline reality. Decisions made from a managerial standpoint might seem effective, but they can often miss the intricacies of frontline operations. For example, a new scheduling system designed to optimise shifts might complicate the daily routines of frontline staff. This misalignment can lead to inefficiencies, dissatisfaction, and a lack of cohesion within the team, or worse still, a team mutiny.

One of the significant challenges for leaders is establishing effective communication channels that enable frontline staff to voice their insights. This feedback is crucial in understanding the challenges and experiences of frontline workers. The challenge lies in creating a culture where this feedback is not just heard but actively sought during the planning process to inform decision-making framework. It's about recognising the value of insights from those who are directly involved in the day-to-day operations of the organisation.

In the intricate weave of an organisation, every person plays a role in maintaining strength and alignment. But when communication breaks down, frontline voices are often the first to be silenced. This leads to well-intentioned strategies that miss the mark—not because they lack merit, but because they lack grounding in reality.

Imagine frontline workers—those who power the organisation's daily operations—watching their concerns vanish like whispers in the wind. Over time, this lack of acknowledgement erodes their sense of value. Morale suffers. And with it, engagement, motivation, and productivity.The absence of clear, consistent communication opens the door to error, inefficiency, and misaligned efforts. It's like a team rowing in different directions—technically in motion, but far from moving forward effectively.To counter this, leaders must create space for open dialogue. This includes setting expectations, recognising good work, and fostering a culture of ongoing coaching and support. Only then can frontline teams grow with clarity and purpose. [1]

The Silent Struggle: The Absence of a Voice for Frontline Workers

Frontline workers are often the unsung heroes of an organisation—the ones who keep everything running. But when they lack a platform to share insights, the result is more than silence. It's lost wisdom.

Their insights are like hidden treasure—valuable, real-world knowledge that often goes unnoticed. Without a positive, structured channel to surface this information, organisations risk walking past opportunities and barreling toward avoidable pitfalls.

Change without input fosters resistance. It's human nature to resist what we don't understand. For frontline teams, change that feels arbitrary can create a sense of disempowerment. It's like being asked to blaze a trail without knowing the destination.

Continuous improvement thrives on feedback. Without it, organisations become blind to what's right in front of them. But when leaders create pathways to capture and act on this feedback, they unlock growth, uncover efficiency, and elevate the entire system.

Leaders can gain these valuable insights through surveys and assessments; leaders can uncover their team's attitudes and actions, gaining clarity on essential dynamics. Armed with this more comprehensive understanding, leaders can develop effective solutions that incorporate employee insights and address the root causes, driving performance improvement, employee engagement, and facilitating overall success.

The significance of developing and nurturing high-performance teams is clear. Such teams are essential not just for their consistent delivery of quality outcomes but also for their substantial role in fostering a positive organisational culture and enhancing engagement.[2].

Coaching isn't a soft-skill luxury—it's a structural necessity. In every industry under pressure, what's failing isn't the strategy. It's the ability to **translate direction into daily behaviour**. That translation happens—or breaks—at the frontline. Most change efforts fall short, not because of poor vision, but because leaders assume people will follow without daily reinforcement. They won't. People don't adapt by instruction; they adapt through conversation, feedback, and belief. That means coaching. But not the kind locked in

HR templates or quarterly reviews. Real coaching—the kind that sticks—is embedded in shift handovers, task checks, walk-arounds and field interactions. When leaders don't coach, teams default. They fill silence with assumption, drift from standard, and wait to be told instead of taking ownership. So coaching isn't what you do after the real work. **It is the real work**—because it's what converts plans into action, and action into habit.

Why should coaching happen at the frontline first. Organisational change often fails because it's planned at the top and hoped for at the bottom. But hope isn't a method. The frontline—where the work is done, standards are tested, and habits are formed—is where belief must be built.Coaching at the frontline is the only scalable way to make leadership visible in the flow of work. Leaders who are present, consistent, and reinforcing what good looks like are the difference between surface compliance and deep capability.

In your role, every instruction carries weight. But it's the follow-up—the tone you use, the question you ask, the habit you reinforce—that determines if your message takes root or gets lost in the noise. Coaching makes leadership repeatable. It shows people not just what's expected, but what matters enough to be checked, praised, or challenged.

If it's not being coached, it's not being led.

Senior leaders can set vision. Systems can set goals. But only the frontline coach can set belief. And belief, not fear or compliance, is what drives performance under pressure.When coaching disappears from the daily rhythm, leaders don't always notice it right away. There's no instant alarm. No urgent red light. But something starts to erode—and by the time you see the performance gap, the damage is already done.Without consistent coaching, **drift happens**. Standards blur. People start doing what feels normal, not what's expected. You'll hear phrases like "we've always done it this way" or "nobody said anything last time," and that's your warning sign: the team has started to coach itself—and usually not in the direction you want.

The result isn't just lower productivity. It's **lower belief**. When leaders go quiet, people start to wonder what really matters. They interpret silence as approval, inconsistency as indifference. The very trust that coaching is supposed to build starts to slip away.

Then come the deeper costs:

- A slowdown in initiative—"I'll just wait to be told."

- A rise in avoidable errors—"No one checks anyway."

- A drop in ownership—"Not my problem anymore."

And when that sets in, it doesn't matter how strong your processes or systems are. If the people doing the work no longer feel seen, supported, or accountable, the system fails quietly. That's why not coaching is never neutral. **It's a signal—one that shapes team culture more than you realise.** Every day you don't coach, the team learns something. The questions are what are they learning?

Strategy on paper means nothing until it meets human behaviour. Most leaders assume that once a plan is announced—new targets, safety campaigns, values—it will be understood and followed. But frontline teams don't operate from PowerPoint decks. They operate from habit, observation, and what they believe their leader values most.

That's where coaching bridges the gap. It doesn't just clarify expectations—it reinforces them in motion. When a leader coaches in the moment ("Show me how you approached that task—what's your thinking?"), they are actively translating the company's direction into behaviour that sticks. This is where trust is built, and alignment becomes real.

In the absence of coaching, people make up their own rules. Not out of rebellion—but out of survival. They do what they think works, what they saw last week, or what doesn't get challenged. Without reinforcement, strategy leaks.And that's the gap: great organisations aren't failing because they lack plans. They're failing because no one's coaching those plans into daily action. Today's work environment isn't getting simpler. More variability, more pressure, more compliance. Whether you're in mining, logistics, healthcare, or manufacturing—**complexity is the norm**, not the exception.

But here's what research and lived experience show: in high-complexity, high-risk environments, performance improves most **when coaching is embedded as a routine response**, not a reactive intervention. In fact, case studies across multiple sectors show a direct correlation between leader visibility, real-time feedback, and operational resilience. Not incidentally—**systematically**. The data is clear: coaching improves clarity, reduces variability, and builds psychological safety. People are more likely to speak up, adjust in real time, and take initiative when they know their leader sees them and engages them. That's because coaching does what no process can do: it affirms that someone is **watching the right things, at the right time, for the right reasons**. And in complex settings, where clarity can collapse under pressure, that matters more than ever.

Chapter 2:

The Shift from Command to Capability

Why command and control isn't building

Many frontline leaders are promoted because they were good at the work. They knew the process, hit their targets, or stood out as reliable. But leading a team is not the same as doing the task. And shouting instructions, checking boxes, or correcting errors in real-time might keep the shift moving—but it doesn't grow the team.

This is the first trap of frontline leadership: believing that authority equals effectiveness. **Telling people what to do is not leadership—it's control. Coaching people to take ownership of what to do is.** Bosses direct effort. Builders shape belief.

Here's how to tell the difference:

Commanding Looks Like...	Building Looks Like...
Why didn't you follow the procedure?	Can we talk through why this part of the procedure exists?
Fixing mistakes personally	Coaching the person to correct it
Issuing orders	Asking questions that spark ownership
Monitoring for failure	Reinforcing small wins and standards

The mindset shift is subtle—but critical. As a boss, your presence drives performance. As a builder, your **coaching makes performance repeatable without you**.

Field Application

Here's how to start shifting from bossing to building:

1. **Pause the directive**: Before telling someone what to do, ask, "What's your approach here?"

2. **Let them speak first**: Even if you already see the issue, let them verbalise their thinking.

3. **Coach the thinking, not just the result**: Reinforce their process, not just whether they got it "right."

4. **End with belief**: Always affirm the capability you see or want to grow—"I trust your judgment here" carries weight.

5. **Audit your language**: Over one shift, track how many times you ask vs tell. The ratio reveals your default leadership mode.

One of the most frustrating things for any leader is inconsistency: a team that performs well one day and under delivers the next. You've given the same instruction. The process hasn't changed. But the result fluctuates. That's not a sign of poor intention. It's a sign of **uncoded behaviours**.

What do we mean by that? Inconsistent teams often rely on memory, habit, and improvisation—rather than shared, coached ways of working. When something goes well, they can't explain why. When something goes wrong, they default to blame or silence. That's not failure—it's drift. And it's preventable.

As a leader-coach, your job is to **code consistency into the team** by reinforcing what good looks like before, during, and after the task. That means going beyond outcomes ("the job's done") and focusing on how it was done—what behaviours created success or caused variation.

Coaching in Practice

Here's how to decode inconsistency using coaching:

1. **Observe patterns, not just events**
   Don't react to isolated failures—look for repeated friction points. Where does performance dip? Is it always at shift handover? With the same equipment? After a specific delay?

2. **Ask: "How did we do that yesterday?"**
   If performance was better last shift, have the team name what they did differently. Make success repeatable by giving it language.

3. **Coach reflection after strong performance**
   We often coach only when things go wrong. But coaching after things go right is how you turn random success into a team standard.

4. **Close the loop with agreed cues**
   Use checklist questions, hand signals, or visual controls that let people self-correct in real time. Teach the team to spot their own variation.

5. **Make standards visible, coachable, and ownable**
   The best teams aren't error-free—they're self-correcting. And that happens when behaviours are clear, expected, and coached consistently.

Some leaders measure a good day by how many tasks got done. On the surface, that looks like performance. Jobs were completed, targets were hit, and no major issues came up.

But here's the trap: **getting the job done doesn't mean the team is getting better**.

Task-only leadership is seductive because it's visible and easy to track. You know what needs doing, and you make sure it gets done. But over time, that approach builds **dependency**, not capability. The leader becomes the bottleneck. The team waits for direction. And initiative quietly fades.

You'll hear it in subtle ways:

- "Just tell me what to do."

- "That's not my call."

- "We've always done it like this."

These aren't just phrases—they're warning signs. They reflect a team that's been trained to comply, not coached to think. And when something changes—new standards, new pressures, or unexpected breakdowns—**task-only teams struggle to adapt**. They follow instructions, but don't respond to context. They wait for answers, even when the answer is already in front of them.

To shift from task-only to capability-focused leadership:

1. **Ask process questions during the task**
   Don't just say, "Do X." Ask: "How are you going to approach it?" This builds decision-making skills.

2. **Coach reflection before you correct**
   When something goes wrong, lead with: "What do you think happened?" You'll grow more from their answer than your own feedback.

3.

4. **Acknowledge behaviour, not just completion**
   Say: "I noticed how you double-checked that clamp before locking in. That's what good looks like." This reinforces the process, not just the outcome.

5. **Use task delivery to build future readiness**
   Every completed task is a coaching moment. Ask: "What would you do differently if the context changed?" This builds range and adaptability.

6. **Track team development, not just throughput**
   Keep a simple log of what each person is learning—not just what they're doing. Over time, this becomes your coaching growth map.

When teams underperform, leaders often look at skills, systems, or workload. But one of the most overlooked drivers of engagement—and by extension, performance—is whether people feel **seen, heard, and valued**.

At the frontline, silence doesn't mean everything is fine. Often, it means people have stopped believing their voice matters. They've tried speaking up before and nothing changed. They've raised ideas and been ignored. Over time, they withdraw. They stop sharing observations, suggestions, or concerns—not because they don't care, but because they no longer think it will make a difference.

As a coach, your job is to reverse that. To create moments where people feel **safe to speak**, confident their input is respected, and clear that their contribution shapes how the team improves. That doesn't mean you say yes to everything. It means you show people they're visible—that what they see, say, and suggest gets acknowledged, tested, and coached.

When people feel heard, they engage. When they feel ignored, they detach. The difference isn't a new program—it's your coaching presence.

Here's how to coach voice, value, and visibility:

1. **Ask open-ended questions daily**
   Instead of "Did you follow the process?" ask: "What stood out to you today?" Create space for insight, not just compliance.

2. **Acknowledge insight in real-time**
   When someone flags a risk, speaks up about a shortcut, or makes a quality catch, name it out loud. It signals to others that voice matters.

3. **Give feedback to the group, not just on the group**
   Say things like, "Here's something I saw that shows we're moving in the right direction…" It reinforces value across the team.

4. **Invite suggestions, then follow through**
   If someone raises a good idea, loop back. Even if it's not adopted, explain why. This builds trust in the process, not just outcomes.

5. **Don't just correct—coach awareness**
   When someone misses something, ask: "What do you think we didn't see there?" This keeps thinking active, even during correction.

When performance breaks down, most leaders rush to fix the task. They retrain the person, rewrite the procedure, or tighten the rule. But real leadership isn't just about reacting—it's about rebuilding the system that allowed the drift to happen in the first place. And coaching is your tool to do that. **Coaching isn't a patch. It's a system reset.** When done consistently, it re-establishes standards, reinforces expectations, and restores belief. And it does so without causing fear, blame, or overdependence. That's the power of coaching: it shifts responsibility to the team without stepping away from leadership.

Think of your team like a system of moving parts—people, processes, pressure, and pace. When one part wobbles, others adjust. But if you coach one piece in isolation and ignore the system, the performance won't hold. To truly rebuild, you need to coach across three layers:

- **Task clarity** – Do they know what "good" looks like?

- **Behaviour alignment** – Are their habits consistent with the standard?

- **Belief reinforcement** – Do they believe the standard matters?

Here's how to rebuild systems through coaching:

1. **Step back before stepping in**
   Don't just fix the problem—scan the system. Ask: "Where else is this showing up?" Drift is rarely isolated.

2. **Coach roles, not just results**
   Reinforce each person's role in holding the system together. "Your check unlocks the next safe step" builds ownership, not dependency.

3. **Make coaching part of the rhythm, not a reaction**
   Don't wait for breakdowns. Use daily moments—handover, tool checks, pre-task talks—as system-check coaching points.

4. **Name the link between standards and outcomes**
   Help people connect their behaviour to real-world impacts. "Because you stopped and checked, we avoided a 2-hour delay."

5. **Use coaching to rebuild belief, not just compliance**
   Ask: "What do you think the standard protects us from?" This shifts people from 'rules' to 'reasons.'

When systems weaken, people fill the gap—or fall through it. Coaching ensures that what's important doesn't drift into silence. It restores what the team believes, what they act on, and what they hold each other to.

Chapter 3:

The Hidden Cost of Not Leading

When leaders stop coaching, things don't collapse overnight. On the surface, the team may still look productive. Tasks get ticked off, shift reports are filed, and targets might even be met. But just beneath that surface, something more fragile is happening—something that doesn't show up on the dashboard but slowly erodes the team's belief, clarity, and trust. "People default to habit under pressure, and habit doesn't change just because a new poster went up."[3]

This gradual erosion is known as *drift*. It doesn't announce itself with noise or immediacy, but it is dangerous nonetheless. Drift begins the moment a team stops hearing what good looks like. When feedback becomes infrequent or inconsistent, people stop checking their performance against a defined standard. Instead, they start making quiet compromises—choosing speed over process, mirroring what they've last observed rather than what was originally taught. Slowly, the gap between "how we're meant to do it" and "how we actually do it" widens. And the more that gap becomes normalised, the harder it is to see—and even harder to correct.

The challenge is that drift feels normal when it's happening. No one thinks they're stepping outside the lines. They're just trying to get the job done. The intention is still good. The work is still happening. But without coaching, small deviations become embedded behaviours. And when those behaviours aren't corrected—or better yet, reinforced when done right—they evolve into the team's new default.

This is where risk creeps in—not just physical or safety risk, but risk to performance, morale, and belief. People start to assume that standards are flexible. That's what matters is speed, not consistency. That no one really notices, so it's fine to cut corners. Coaching is what holds the line. Without it, the line doesn't just bend—it disappears.

So while the absence of coaching might not cause immediate failure, it guarantees a slow, silent shift away from everything the team was built to deliver. And once that shift becomes the norm, pulling it back into alignment becomes twice the effort. Because now you're not just correcting behaviour—you're rebuilding belief.

The cost of not coaching is rarely listed on a balance sheet, but it shows up everywhere. It lives in the hesitation of a team member who used to speak up but now stays silent. It creeps into the handover that's rushed and incomplete because no one asks the second question anymore. It's there in the dropped standard that goes unchallenged, simply because "no one said anything." And over time, that silence becomes systemic.

Disengagement doesn't always announce itself. It often arrives looking like obedience. The job still gets done, but there's no energy behind it. No ownership. People do what's asked, but nothing more. They wait to be told, even when they already know what to do. Initiative fades. Confidence erodes. Eventually, good people begin to check out—not because they don't care, but because the feedback loop has collapsed. If no one's reinforcing the value of their effort, why push harder?

Disruption is the next layer. Without coaching to stabilise standards and reinforce the right behaviours, teams become reactive. They stop thinking ahead. They firefight, escalate, and work around problems rather than solving them. Relationships suffer. Trust fractures. And soon, energy that should be spent improving the system is now spent surviving it.Drift is the silent partner of disengagement and disruption. It happens when a once-strong team gradually starts operating on assumptions instead of alignment. They think they're still doing the right thing, but no one's verifying. No one's reinforcing. The team has drifted—not just from standard, but from belief.

And this is the real cost. Not just in safety incidents, missed targets, or rework—though those will come. The deeper cost is the loss of a team's inner momentum. That sense of rhythm and clarity that once allowed them to operate with pride, speed, and shared accountability. Coaching isn't just about correcting people. It's about keeping that rhythm alive. Because when it goes quiet, everything else starts to fall out of step.

There's a common belief in many organisations that once change has been communicated, it's ready to be implemented. The email goes out, the new standard is explained, the briefing is held—and with that, the assumption is made: the team is now ready. But readiness isn't a function of how clearly change is announced. It's a function of how consistently it's reinforced.

This is the myth that derails so many well-meaning initiatives. Leaders assume that because something was explained, it was absorbed. That because something was taught, it was understood. And that because it was rolled out, it will now be followed. In reality, change only becomes real when it's lived—and that only happens when leaders coach it into motion.

Without coaching, change is treated like a one-time event, not a shift in how people think, act, and respond. Teams may nod in agreement during the rollout, but the moment pressure returns—when time is short, when equipment fails, when the supervisor isn't nearby—they revert to what feels safe and familiar. That's not resistance. That's human behaviour. Change-readiness is not about understanding. It's about **belief reinforced by coaching**. Belief that this new way is not only expected but supported. That it's safe to try, to ask, to make mistakes, and to improve. That someone will notice, guide, and course-correct—not punish, instruct, or walk away.

A leader who doesn't coach through change is like a builder who leaves the scaffolding up halfway. The structure looks solid from a distance, but it can't hold weight. Without reinforcement, change remains a surface-level adjustment. It may show up in reports, but it doesn't last in practice. The frontline doesn't need more change announcements. It needs more coaching moments that say: this is real, this is supported, and this is ours to own

The most dangerous risks in any operation aren't always the ones listed on the risk register. They're the ones that live in plain sight—hidden in the gap between what's expected and what's actually happening. The skipped step that's become routine. The half-completed check that no one follows up on. The assumption that "it's fine because nothing went wrong last time." These are the kinds of risks that don't show up in audits until something breaks.

That's what makes them dangerous: they're not invisible because they're hidden. They're invisible because they've become normal.

This is where coaching proves its value—not just as a tool for development, but as a **protective force** inside your system. Coaching surfaces assumptions. It draws attention to the space between intention and behaviour. It brings small habits into view before they become major failures. In a world where many risks are behavioural and cultural, coaching becomes the frontline's most reliable detection system.

What makes coaching effective is its precision. It doesn't rely on generic warnings or blanket reminders. It's built on observation, questioning, and feedback in the moment. It says, "Show me how you're doing this," not "Make sure you do it right." That small shift changes everything. Because it reveals, clarifies, and recalibrates—before a problem has the chance to embed itself.

The teams that perform consistently under pressure aren't just technically skilled. They're coached into clarity. They've had their habits stress-tested and their blind spots exposed in a way that feels safe. They're used to being asked why—not just what. And that culture of regular, visible coaching keeps risk from becoming routine.

You don't need perfect systems to manage risk. You need leaders who stay close enough to see it coming—and who coach early enough to stop it from settling in.

When leaders don't coach, the consequences don't always show up in a single event. They accumulate—quietly and gradually—until what once felt strong begins to fall apart. Coaching, done consistently, doesn't just build capability. It protects against the slow decay that happens when no one is watching the right things, asking the right questions, or reinforcing the right behaviours.

The first thing to erode is **clarity**. Without regular coaching, standards lose their edge. What was once clearly defined becomes negotiable. People start doing things the way they remember, or the way the last person showed them. The intention is still there, but the consistency is gone. This erosion rarely happens with defiance. It happens with the slow fading of reinforcement.

Next come the **excuses**. In the absence of coaching, accountability turns into avoidance. Teams begin to justify short cuts or underperformance because, over time, the leader stopped holding the line. You'll hear things like "We weren't trained properly," or "We just do what we can with what we've got." These aren't signs of laziness—they're symptoms of a coaching vacuum. Without feedback and support, people start protecting themselves instead of improving.

Eventually, people don't just step back from the work—they **step away from the belief** that it matters. That's when the exit begins. Sometimes literally, as good people leave roles where they no longer feel seen or developed. More often, though, the exit is emotional. People stay in the job, but check out of the work. They stop showing initiative, stop offering input, and stop growing. That silent resignation is what drains team momentum the most—and it's hard to measure until the damage is done.But all of this can be prevented.

Coaching is how leaders hold the line on belief. It's how they keep the standard real, the conversations open, and the team anchored in a shared sense of direction. Without it, erosion is inevitable. With it, teams not only stay aligned— they grow stronger with time.

Chapter 4:

Leadership Behaviours That Stick

At the frontline, tasks are everywhere—starting pumps, checking gauges, preparing materials, executing isolations. Most get done. But there's a world of difference between **a task that's completed and one that's completed to standard.** That gap is where quality either holds—or slips.

Doing the task is the minimum. Doing it to standard is the behaviour that sustains safe, reliable, and efficient operations. And that's why it's the first, and most fundamental, behaviour to coach.

What it looks like:
A person executes a task with attention to the defined process—steps followed in order, checks performed properly, conditions verified, and the job signed off with traceability and pride. There's no skipping, rushing, or guessing. It's done properly—even when no one is watching.

What it signals:
This behaviour tells you that the person understands not just what to do, but why it must be done a certain way. It reflects ownership, respect for process, and a belief that quality matters. When repeated, it creates reliability. When coached, it becomes culture.

Why it matters:
Standards exist for a reason. In mining, manufacturing, logistics—wherever you work—standards are what protect people, assets, and continuity. Every time someone cuts a step, the standard weakens. When enough people do it, the system fails. Coaching this behaviour protects the system before it breaks.

How to coach it:
 Be present during execution. Don't just wait for the outcome—watch the process. Ask questions like:

- •"What's your first check before starting this?"

- "Why do we follow this particular sequence?"

- "How do you know you've completed this task to spec?"

Use language that reinforces precision and pride, not just speed. Don't reward rushed work—praise thorough work done right the first time.

What happens when it's missing:
You start seeing inconsistency in results. Variability increases. Mistakes become harder to trace. Blame starts to creep in. "I thought someone else checked it." "We don't usually bother with that step." These are not failures of intelligence. They're failures of reinforcement. And it starts when leaders stop coaching the difference between done and done right.

A task handover isn't a formality—it's a control point. And yet, across many frontline environments, handovers are treated as routine checkboxes: "Job's done." "All good." "You're up." These aren't handovers. They're shortcuts. And when shortcuts become habits, information gets lost—and so does accountability.

A true handover includes **context**. Not just what was done, but what's still in motion. What changed, what didn't, what went wrong, what to watch for, and what support is needed to continue safely and effectively. It connects the previous shift to the next and keeps the system coherent. This is a coachable behaviour—and it's a vital one.

What it looks like:
The outgoing team or individual communicates more than task status. They explain what's been completed, any deviations, pending hazards, current readings, and next steps. They check understanding. They don't just pass the job—they pass the full picture.

What it signals:
This behaviour tells you someone takes ownership not just of what they did but of how their actions impact what happens next. It shows pride, foresight, and team orientation. When done consistently, it creates flow. When skipped, it creates fragmentation.

Why it matters:
Poor handovers are a root cause of many frontline failures—missed inspections, incorrect settings, unsafe restarts, duplicated work. They aren't caused by malice. They're caused by assumptions. And assumptions thrive where coaching is absent.

How to coach it:
Observe handovers regularly. Don't just ask, "Was the job handed over?" Ask:

- "What context did you give them?"

- "What risks are still open?"

- "How did you confirm they understood?"

Coach team members to slow down and share the why, not just the what. Use reflection after incidents to highlight where context was missed. Build in structured prompts or handover sheets if needed—but never let the form replace the conversation.

What happens when it's missing:
Gaps appear. A valve left unmonitored. A hazard unflagged. A shift that restarts from the wrong baseline. Small issues compound. And slowly, people stop trusting handovers altogether—choosing instead to recheck everything or ignore the input altogether. This wastes time, breaks rhythm, and erodes trust between shifts.

Coaching this behaviour isn't optional—it's foundational. Because a handover without context isn't a handover. It's a delay waiting to happen.

One of the most dangerous habits in any operational environment is assumption. It doesn't start as recklessness—it starts as confidence. A pump sounds fine, so it must be running correctly. A tag is present, so isolation must be complete. A task looks simple, so the risk must be low. But in complex systems, what's assumed often goes unchecked. And what goes unchecked eventually goes wrong.

Verification is not a sign of doubt—it's a behaviour of discipline. It says: I trust the system, but I check anyway. I respect the process, so I confirm. That's not overkill. That's how professionals operate under pressure.

This is a coachable behaviour—and one of the most protective ones you can reinforce.

What it looks like:
A team member actively confirms the key controls before proceeding. They ask to see the permit. They walk down the area themselves. They check equipment tags, pressure levels, temperatures, or procedures without relying on second-hand updates. They don't assume someone else got it right—they take ownership for what they're about to step into.

What it signals:
This behaviour reflects **maturity, risk awareness, and respect for consequence**. It tells you this person isn't rushing to prove they're capable—they're committed to doing things right. When this shows up consistently, it becomes part of your safety culture, your quality control, and your reliability assurance.

Why it matters:
Many incidents—minor and major—start from a simple point of failure: someone assumed instead of checked. And those assumptions are often made by skilled, experienced people who've "done it a hundred times." That's exactly why coaching matters. Because overconfidence and complacency aren't corrected by training. They're corrected

by leadership presence—and reinforcement of verification as a non-negotiable behaviour.

How to coach it:
Use field walks, job observations, and handovers as coaching moments. When you see someone checking, name it and reinforce it: "I saw you walk that line before trusting the valve was isolated—that's how we stay safe."

When you don't see checking, don't ignore it. Pause the work. Ask:

- "What have you verified personally?"

- "What information did you base that decision on?"

- "What would you check if this was your first time doing it?"

Don't turn this into interrogation. Turn it into expectation. Make verification a point of pride.

What happens when it's missing:
Teams start shortcutting controls. Visual checks disappear. Paperwork becomes assumed. Near misses increase. And soon, problems that could've been caught early escalate into breakdowns, exposures, or failures. The team gets faster, but the system gets weaker.

Without coaching, people assume. With coaching, people check. And that small difference is what keeps operations resilient.

Owning the Outcome—Following Through Beyond the Task

In high-performing teams, the job isn't done when the last step is ticked off. It's done when the outcome is confirmed, the impact is understood, and the team is ready for what comes next. That's the difference between executing a task and **owning its outcome**.

Ownership is not about doing more. It's about caring more about what your task leads to. It's the behaviour that drives someone to check whether their isolation actually enabled the maintenance crew to start work safely. To follow up on a checklist not just to complete it, but to ensure that the action taken achieved what it was meant to. To hand something over—and then ask later how it went.

This behaviour matters because performance doesn't end at the individual task level. Every piece of work connects to another. Systems are built on flow. And flow depends on people who think beyond their task and care about the total picture.

What it looks like:
A person completes their task and then checks downstream. They ask the next operator if the output was right. They follow up after handover to confirm it landed. They reflect on how their work affected others. They don't wait for problems—they pre-empt them. Not because they have to, but because they care.

What it signals:
This behaviour shows **belief in contribution and commitment to quality**. It reflects someone who understands that doing the job isn't the goal—making the system work is. It tells you they've shifted from task mindset to team mindset. And that's exactly what sustainable performance requires.

Why it matters:
Too often, problems emerge not because people didn't do their jobs—but because they didn't follow through. No one noticed that the task didn't land where it needed to. No one checked that the expected outcome actually materialised. And by the time it's noticed, the delay or the defect has spread downstream. Coaching follow-through turns "I did my part" into "I made sure it worked."

How to coach it:
Ask questions that push the boundary beyond task:

- "What did your work enable for the next team?"

- "How do you know the result was effective?"

- "What happened after you completed your part?"

Recognise this behaviour when you see it. Say things like: "Following up like that shows real ownership." Don't just praise completion—praise outcome awareness.

What happens when it's missing:
You get fragmented performance. Each person does their part, but no one owns the flow. Issues get handed off instead of solved. Teams shift from proactive to reactive. Eventually, work becomes mechanical—and problems start living in the spaces between people. That's when frustration rises, trust erodes, and finger-pointing begins.

Coaching this behaviour builds pride. Not just in doing the job—but in seeing it through. That's what high-performing, resilient teams are made of.In most operational environments, the earliest warning signs of trouble don't come from systems—they come from people. Someone notices a subtle change in noise, a delay in pressure, a shortcut in prep, or a conversation that doesn't feel right. These signals show up long before breakdowns or incidents. But they only make a difference **if someone speaks up—and someone listens**.

Encouraging people to raise flags early is not about creating paranoia. It's about building a culture where observation and voice are treated as professional responsibilities—not emotional risks. It's about saying: if you see something, we want to hear it. And more than that—we'll act on it.This is a coachable behaviour. And when it's not coached, silence becomes a learned habit.

What it looks like:
A team member highlights an inconsistency or potential issue without waiting to be asked. They raise their hand when they're unsure, call out a potential clash in permits, or

mention a missing component that could delay the job. They don't wait for permission. They treat early escalation as part of doing the job right.

What it signals:
This behaviour reflects **psychological safety, system thinking, and personal responsibility**. It shows that someone feels empowered to act in the interest of the whole—not just their part. When it becomes normal, the team becomes anticipatory, not reactive.

Why it matters:
Many near misses—and actual incidents—could have been prevented if someone had spoken up earlier. But speaking up feels risky if leaders don't coach and reward it. Without reinforcement, people interpret silence as safer than being wrong. They start saying things like "It wasn't my place," or "I didn't want to slow things down." Coaching breaks that cycle.

How to coach it:
When someone speaks up—especially if it turns out to be a false alarm—acknowledge the courage. Say: "That's exactly the kind of thinking we want." Use examples from past events to show where early voice could have made a difference. And model the behaviour yourself—share what you're watching out for.

Ask regularly:

- "What feels off here?"

- "If this task were to go wrong, where would it start?"

- "Is there anything we're assuming that we haven't checked?"

Make it clear that speaking up early isn't a disruption. It's part of the flow. It's what professionals do.

What happens when it's missing:
Issues build in the background. Opportunities to prevent are missed. Trust weakens because people feel they can't raise concerns without consequence. Eventually, teams get used to living with friction, noise, and risk—until something breaks. By then, it's too late. And the team that could've stopped it now carries the weight of silence.

Coaching this behaviour is how you move from firefighting to foresight. From "Why didn't anyone say anything?" to "Good call—you saved us a step."

The behaviours in this chapter aren't just "nice to have." They are the **operating foundation of a high-performing team**. Each one represents a moment where performance can either reinforce belief and consistency—or slide into drift, confusion, and rework.

These behaviours are key because they are:

- **Visible** – You can see them in action.

- **Coachable** – You can reinforce or redirect them in the moment.

- **Cumulative** – They shape the culture not just individually, but collectively.

- **Consequential** – When done well, they protect the system. When neglected, they quietly weaken it.

Left unchecked, these habits don't just affect one job—they cascade. A rushed handover leads to a missed step. A missed step leads to a delayed outcome. A delay sparks frustration. Frustration erodes ownership. And suddenly, what started as a minor behaviour gap has become a cultural norm.

The intent of coaching these behaviours is simple: **to build belief, clarity, and ownership into daily work**. Coaching turns expectations into action, and action into habit. It makes invisible standards visible again. It creates accountability without aggression. And most importantly, it gives leaders a practical, repeatable way to shape performance in real time—without relying on reports or escalation. The goal is not perfection. The goal is **consistency in the right direction**. Because when you coach these behaviours, you're not just improving the task—you're reinforcing the system behind it. This is how leadership becomes real. Not through position or policy—but through the quiet, daily act of helping people do the right thing, the right way, for the right reason.

PART 2:

BUILD YOUR TOOLKIT

Chapter 5:

Leading with Insight Builds Capability

If coaching was only about giving feedback, most teams would be high-performing by now. But here's the reality: most coaching conversations don't stick. They're too fast, too top-down, or too focused on the problem instead of the person. The moment passes, and so does the insight. And the same issue shows up again next week.

The problem isn't the leader's intent. It's the structure. Or more accurately, the lack of one. Without a rhythm to guide the conversation, coaching becomes either correction or encouragement—but rarely growth. That's why most feedback ends in a nod, not a change. It may feel clear in the moment, but it doesn't move belief. And belief is what drives behaviour when no one's watching.

This is where reflective coaching becomes different. It's not about telling someone what they did right or wrong. It's about creating a space where they think it through, feel the consequence, and name their own next move. That's what creates ownership. Because insight doesn't land when it's delivered—it lands when it's discovered.

The shift is subtle, but powerful:
From giving answers → To asking better questions
From leader-led judgment → To co-owned reflection
From coaching as correction → To coaching as capability building

This approach works because it changes the conversation sequence. Instead of diving straight into what you saw, it begins with what they saw. That small reordering slows the conversation down just enough to open a learning moment. And in fast-paced environments, that's a skill that sets leaders apart—not because it's flashy, but because it works. The truth is, coaching doesn't have to be complicated. But it does need to be structured. Not scripted. Not robotic. Just consistent enough to create belief, and flexible enough to meet the moment. The Reflective Coaching Method does exactly that.

And the best part? You already have the moments. You're already walking the floor, reviewing work, talking at the toolbox. All you need now is the sequence that turns those moments into momentum. Great coaching doesn't happen because you said the right thing—it happens because the right thing landed. And for that to happen, the person being coached has to process the moment, not just receive it. That's where the power of sequence comes in.

The Reflective Coaching Method uses five simple steps. They aren't revolutionary. But they are intentional. They're structured to move the person from surface awareness to real insight—and from insight to self-owned action. They're structured to move the person from surface awareness to real insight—and from insight to self-owned action.[4]

It starts with a pause: **"How do you think you went?"**
This is not small talk. It's a door. It breaks the pattern of leader monologue and asks the person to step into the coaching moment with agency. When you lead with this, you send a message: your thinking matters here. And that changes how they listen from that point forward.

Next: **"What do you think you did well?"**
This isn't about fluff. It's about recognising repeatable success. Most people overlook their strengths—especially when they're under pressure. This question helps them name what worked. And naming is what makes it teachable. If they can't describe what they did well, they can't repeat it. If they can, they've just reinforced their own growth.

Then comes the stretch: **"What didn't go well?"**
This is where most leaders jump in too early. But by now, the person has spoken twice—and that builds trust. When you ask this third, it's not a trap. It's a prompt. They've been

invited to reflect, not defend. And often, you'll be surprised—they'll name the gap before you need to.

Now the pivot: **"What was the impact?"**
This is the question that turns behaviour into consequence. It connects actions to outcomes—safety, time, quality, flow. It builds systems thinking. Because it's not enough to know what went wrong; they need to feel why it matters.

And finally: **"What will you do differently next time?"**
This is where the growth locks in. Not because you prescribed it—but because they chose it. That's where ownership begins. If the person can name their next move, they're far more likely to make it real. And you're not left holding the change—they are.

That's the sequence. Reflect → Achieve → Discover → Impact → Improve. It doesn't need to be formal. It doesn't need a form. It just needs to become your habit.

Use it walking between sites. Use it after a small mistake. Use it when something goes right and you want to make it stick. The more you practice this sequence, the more natural it becomes—not just for you, but for your team. And over time, this rhythm becomes your leadership fingerprint: calm, consistent, developmental.

Because when coaching becomes a rhythm, growth becomes inevitable.

Coaching isn't something you schedule once a month or reserve for formal reviews. It's a leadership behaviour that lives inside your everyday rhythm. The best leaders don't wait for the perfect moment—they make the moment count. And they understand that the most powerful coaching happens during the work, not just after it. The best leaders don't wait for the perfect moment—they make the moment count.[5]

You coach when a task is fresh—when the behaviour is still recent enough to reflect on, but not so far gone that the learning has faded. That might be right after a job's completed, during a shift handover, or even as something starts to drift mid-task. These moments are short, but they're potent. And the leader who's paying attention knows when to pause, lean in, and guide the reflection.

But timing is only part of what makes coaching work. The other part—just as critical—is **how you show up**. If your tone feels evaluative, people get defensive. If your questions feel like a test, they'll shut down. But if your presence feels steady—genuinely curious, not corrective—something different happens. People open up. They think. They self-adjust.

And that's the real goal of coaching: not to correct behaviour after the fact, but to **create the kind of reflection that changes behaviour next time.**

What makes coaching stick is repetition with safety. It's the leader who makes this a normal part of the day. Not a special event. Not a disciplinary moment. Just something we do—because we care about how we grow, not just how we perform.If you've coached someone three or four times using the same reflective sequence, something clicks. They begin to self-initiate the pattern. They start asking themselves those same five questions. That's when you know you're no longer delivering coaching—you've embedded it.

And if you've ever wondered whether it's worth the time— just watch what happens over three weeks. Teams coached in rhythm start owning their gaps. They start catching each other early. They begin to expect feedback—not fear it. That's not soft culture. That's performance sustainability. So when should you coach? When something stands out. When something slips. When something lands well. Or simply, when someone's ready to grow. Because the real coaching moment isn't about what just happened. It's about what happens next. And that moment is always yours to create.

Even the most committed leaders miss coaching moments. Not because they don't care—but because pressure speeds things up. Tasks get stacked, handovers get squeezed, and what could have been a turning point becomes just another

"I'll talk to them later." But later rarely comes. And when it does, the moment is cold.

Here's the truth most leaders learn the hard way: **you don't need more time to coach—you need to stop walking past the moments that already exist.** Coaching doesn't fail because you didn't have a formal sit-down. It fails because a small behavioural cue went unacknowledged. A mistake went unspoken. A great decision went unreinforced. And when those signals go unnoticed too many times, your team stops sending them.

The most common miss is this: the leader assumes the person knows. They assume the team member knows what went wrong, or knows what they did well, or knows how it impacted the work. But assumption is the enemy of coaching. If you don't surface it, they don't own it. And if they don't own it, they can't grow from it.

Another miss: jumping in with feedback before reflection. It feels efficient—"Let me just tell you what to fix"—but it skips the most important part. People don't learn by being told. They learn by seeing it for themselves. If you speak before they've had a chance to think, you've done the work for them. They may agree with you, but they won't grow because of you.So how do you recover a missed moment?

You name it. You go back, even if it's later that day or early the next. You say: "I missed a chance to walk through that job with you yesterday. Let's take five minutes—I want to hear how you thought it went." That one sentence reopens the door. It shows presence. It shows intent. And it shows humility—something teams respect far more than constant direction.

Great coaches aren't perfect—they're consistent. They don't try to catch every moment, but they do recognise when they've missed one worth revisiting. More importantly, they embed those moments into the culture. When teams understand that reflection is a normal part of how work is done, they begin to seek it. They come to expect it. And that's when coaching shifts—from being a leader-driven intervention to becoming a team-led evolution. You can feel when coaching is working. It doesn't show up as a dramatic shift or a sudden breakthrough. It reveals itself in quieter ways—in the clarity that appears in someone's eyes when they connect their behaviour to a deeper purpose than just completing the task. It's in the nod that signals understanding. In the thoughtful pause before action. In the follow-through that no longer needs to be chased.

The moment coaching lands, a switch flips. And it's almost never about the task. It's about belief. The person starts showing up with a different energy—not louder, not flashier, just more anchored. They make better decisions, not because they were told to, but because they now understand the ripple effect. They care about how their actions impact others. They take that extra five seconds to verify, to clarify, to finish strong. And they do it without being reminded.

For the leader, something shifts too. You stop chasing. You start seeing your team take accountability before you step in. You start hearing your own coaching words echoed back in team discussions—recycled, adapted, owned. That's when you know coaching has moved from method to mindset. It doesn't mean performance becomes perfect. But it does become self-correcting. Teams recover faster. They speak more honestly. They take pride not just in getting through the day, but in how they work together through it.

That's what coaching changes. And that's why it matters. Because in the end, coaching isn't just a skill you develop. It's a belief you hold: That people are capable of growing when given the space to think, the safety to speak, and the structure to act. And when leaders commit to that belief—not once, but daily—they don't just change performance. They change people.

Chapter 6:

Growth That Happens on the Job

Most leaders believe in coaching—but they wait too long to do it. Not because they're lazy or disinterested, but because they're waiting for the right moment: when things are calmer, when the shift is done, when there's more time to think it through. That moment rarely comes.

If you're waiting for coaching to be convenient, it will never happen.

Frontline work is unpredictable. Equipment fails. People call in sick. Priorities shift. That means your leadership rhythm can't depend on stillness. It has to work in motion. And coaching—if it's going to be effective—has to live inside the pace, not outside it.

The idea that coaching needs a quiet room, a cup of coffee, or a scheduled one-on-one is a myth. The most effective coaching moments happen in the middle of the task, just after a decision, or right before something gets repeated the wrong way. They're short, often casual, and easily missed if you're not paying attention. But they're the ones that stick.

This is where leadership maturity kicks in. You don't need to prepare a speech. You just need to be present, observe what's happening, and ask a better question. This is where leadership maturity kicks in. Because the moment might not feel perfect, but if someone is making a decision, taking a shortcut, finishing a job, or walking away from a conversation—that's your window [6].

Leaders who coach in motion don't wait for alignment—they create it. And they do it without stopping the work. They're not pulling people off the floor—they're leaning in for 30 seconds to say, "Talk me through your decision there."

They're walking the floor not just to inspect, but to confirm, reinforce, and build belief. Not later—now. Because the real cost of waiting isn't just missed growth. It's drift. And every time you delay coaching, the team gets better at working without it. That's not just a lost moment—it's a rehearsal for inconsistency. The perfect coaching moment is the one in front of you. Take it.

Coaching in the flow isn't just convenient—it's powerful. It works because it meets people where they are, in the real conditions they're facing, with the behaviours they're currently displaying. There's no abstraction, no memory gap, no theoretical detour. It's immediate, personal, and relevant. That's what gives it power. You're not talking about behaviour—you're inside it. You're not recalling a moment—you're capturing it while it's still warm.

Behaviour sticks best when it's reinforced inside the same rhythm it was formed in. If someone cuts a corner at 9:07am and you coach it at 3pm in an office, you've already missed the impact window. The lesson might still land, but it has to travel further. But if you coach it right there—where the sound, pressure, pace, and tension are still real—it's different. The insight lands in the nervous system, not just the notebook.

Teams coached in motion learn faster because the feedback is attached to actual work. There's no leap. No translation needed. You're not asking them to imagine a better response—you're helping them see it in the moment they're living through.

The signals go both ways. When your team sees you coaching in real time—not only when something goes wrong, but when something goes right—it tells them what matters. It tells them that coaching isn't a reaction to failure. It's a rhythm of growth. It tells them you're watching for belief, not just compliance. That creates safety. And from safety comes initiative.

Coaching in the flow also shifts identity. The team stops seeing you as the person who shows up with corrections.

They start seeing you as the person who helps them think. That's when trust deepens. That's when conversations get honest. That's when people start saying, "Can I get your eyes on this?" before the job is even finished. Researchers in high-reliability environments have found that coaching or feedback delivered during real-time task execution—rather than after the fact—leads to higher behavioural retention, faster learning, and stronger team performance[7]. And all of that comes from coaching in moments that others walk past.

This kind of coaching doesn't slow you down. It makes you sharper. Because when the team is being developed in motion, you spend less time firefighting later. Less time revisiting old issues. Less time fixing what was never coached.

It's not about volume—it's about **velocity with intention**. Coaching in the flow creates a performance rhythm that reinforces itself. And once that rhythm is felt, the system begins to improve without you needing to push it. That's not micromanagement. That's leadership by presence.

You don't need to invent time to coach. You just need to recognise the moments that are already part of your day—and decide to use them differently. Because leadership at the frontline isn't about carving out hours for development chats. It's about weaving coaching into the flow of work, using the natural pulse of your shift.

Take the **prestart or toolbox talk**. Most of the time, it's used to deliver updates, tick off hazard discussions, and move on. But it can be so much more. It's your first chance to coach belief before tasks begin. A 30-second prompt like, "What will we need to slow down for today?" invites reflection. It doesn't delay the shift—it sharpens the team. And when done daily, it sets a tone: thinking comes before moving.

During task execution, the work itself offers constant coaching windows. Watch how someone prepares. How they check their equipment. How they speak to a teammate.

These moments are full of signals. Coaching doesn't need to stop the job. A simple: "What made you choose that order?" or "What's your check before you lock out?" keeps the person in control, but raises their awareness. That's reinforcement in real time.

Handovers are another rich opportunity. Don't treat them as just a status transfer. Ask: "What was the biggest judgment call you made during this shift?" or "What's the one thing you'd want the next person to double-check?" This deepens ownership and signals that you're coaching not just task flow—but decision flow.

Even **walk-throughs** or informal check-ins can become coaching touchpoints. Most leaders use these to look for non-compliance. But if you shift your lens, they become opportunities to see who's reinforcing the standard—and who's drifting. When you spot either, name it. That moment matters more than any policy reminder could.

Don't underestimate **after-action conversations**. Whether something went wrong or went brilliantly, the reflection window is short—but powerful. Take 90 seconds to ask: "What surprised you?" or "What will you carry into next time?" That's where learning locks in.None of this requires more paperwork. It doesn't require a coaching diary or weekly sit-downs. It just requires presence and the intent to turn moments into momentum.

The rhythm is already there. The opportunity is already built in. All you need to do is choose to lead through it—one conversation at a time. One of the most common concerns from frontline leaders is this: "I want to coach more, but I can't afford to slow the team down." It's an honest tension. When time is tight and the board is full, coaching can feel like a luxury—something to do later, when things calm down. But that mindset is exactly what keeps teams stuck in firefighting mode.

Coaching doesn't compete with execution. It **protects** it. It builds capability so you don't have to double-handle, chase mistakes, or repeat instructions three times in a week. It slows things down once so they run faster every time after.

That's the shift:
From seeing coaching as a delay → To using coaching as a performance accelerator
From adding coaching to your workload → To building coaching into how you lead

Let's be clear—coaching isn't a speech. It's a **cue**. A moment of reflection. A redirection with context. It takes less time than fixing rework or writing up an incident report. It's not a pause—it's a pivot. And when you learn to deliver it inside the flow, the team starts to absorb it like oxygen. It becomes part of how they think, not something extra they're given.

If a team is waiting for instructions, that's time to coach. If someone finishes early and shrugs, that's time to coach. If a shortcut worked this time, that's especially the time to coach—because silent wins based on drift are the riskiest ones of all. And coaching in those moments doesn't stop the job. It **steers** it.

Leaders often fear they'll lose momentum by coaching. But the deeper truth is this: when you don't coach, you lose alignment. And every degree of misalignment costs more time than you think—through handover friction, task duplication, missed checks, or quiet disengagement.

So here's the ask: don't wait for the day to calm down. Don't wait for the team to struggle. Use what's already in front of you. Start small. One moment. One comment. One question that redirects attention to behaviour and belief.

Because when coaching becomes natural, performance becomes stable. And when performance stabilises, that's when you get your time back.

If coaching only happens when there's time, it'll never become real. But if it happens because it's part of how you lead—every day, in small moments, with consistent intent—then it doesn't just stick. It multiplies.

That's the point of coaching in the flow of work. Not to add more to your plate, but to build habits that **free you from chasing the basics**. Because the more your team grows, the more they begin to self-correct. They reflect before you ask. They notice each other's behaviours. They carry the standard when you're not in the room. And that starts with your habit—not theirs. Studies of sustained leadership routines across healthcare and manufacturing environments show that embedding coaching moments within operational flow leads to stronger habit formation, faster team alignment, and reduced supervisory burden over time [8].

Your daily coaching rhythm doesn't need to be fancy. It needs to be **intentional**. Choose one anchor per shift: a walk-through, a handover, a reset moment after a task. Use that moment every day, without fail. Don't overthink it. Just show up with a coaching lens.

That lens might sound like:

- "What worked well for you just now?"

- "What would you change next time?"

- "What are we walking into that's different today?"

These aren't performance reviews. They're leadership touchpoints. Repeated just enough to create expectation. Reinforced just enough to shape belief. This is how culture forms—not in one big moment, but in dozens of small ones that repeat.

And here's the shift you'll see over time: your team will stop looking at you for answers, and start looking at you for thinking space. They'll bring you questions. They'll come back with insight. They'll expect to reflect—because that's just how we work here.

That's when coaching moves from something you do to something you are. Not a tool you apply, but a way you lead.

So set the rhythm. One moment per day. One behaviour at a time. Make coaching normal—so growth becomes expected.

Coaching isn't something you wait to do. It's something you build into how you lead.

This chapter wasn't about adding new work. It was about seeing what's already there—moments during handovers, walk-throughs, toolbox talks, or just after a job is done—and using them with purpose. These aren't interruptions. They're invitations to shape belief, reinforce standard, and lock in behaviours that hold under pressure. When coaching happens in motion, it lands deeper. The task is still fresh. The pressure is still real. The feedback sticks because it's attached to the work. You're not pulling people out of their world—you're stepping into it with them. That's why it works. And when done consistently, coaching becomes a rhythm. The team expects it. They start reflecting before you ask. They start reinforcing each other. And your role shifts from correcting drift to reinforcing alignment.

This is the turning point. Coaching isn't a task to tick off. It's your leadership fingerprint. And when it becomes part of your daily rhythm, it does more than improve performance. It builds belief. It strengthens trust. And it creates a team that can grow—with or without you standing over them. Because when you lead through coaching—not sometimes, but every day—the work gets better, the thinking gets sharper, and the standard becomes real.

Chapter 7:

Bringing Standards to Life

Respect isn't a coaching technique. It's the foundation of coaching that works.

A respectful approach doesn't mean being soft, indirect, or overly careful. It means treating the person across from you as capable, adult, and worth developing. It means assuming competence before proving fault—and creating a tone that invites growth, not compliance.

In frontline environments, where pressure is high and the pace is unforgiving, it's easy for leaders to fall into command mode. You see something wrong, you step in fast. You give the fix. You move on. But what gets missed in that urgency is the invisible residue—the message left behind that says: "I don't trust you to think." That message, whether intended or not, corrodes belief. Not just in the task—but in the system and the leader delivering it.

That's why great coaches begin from a posture of respect.
They approach with **permission**, not force.
They say:

> "Mind if I offer something on that last step?"
> Or:
> "Would it help to think that through together?"

This doesn't weaken authority—it strengthens connection. When you ask before entering someone's performance space, you signal: "I trust that you care about getting this right. I'm here to support that—not override it." This tone matters even more when the conversation is corrective. If someone's made a mistake or overlooked a standard, the instinct might be to assert authority quickly. But a respectful approach holds the line without crushing the person. It creates space for ownership to emerge—on its own.

It might sound like:

> "I noticed something I'd like to check with you.
> Can we step through the process together?"

What you're doing is disarming shame before it can take root. You're keeping the conversation grounded in process, not personality. And that tone creates the conditions for real learning—because the person stays open, not guarded [9].Respect also means recognising the effort that went into the task, even if the outcome missed the mark. Acknowledge the context. Validate the challenge. Then coach the behaviour

"I know that step was time-pressured—and you still took the right precaution. That's what I want to reinforce."

This isn't flattery—it's reinforcement. It helps the person recognise that standards aren't optional under pressure; they are essential because of it. Respect is communicated not just through words, but through body language, tone, and physical stance. Are you standing beside the person or over them? Are your hands open or crossed? Is your voice calm or curt? These signals carry meaning. People often remember how a coaching moment *felt* more than the exact words used. And those emotional impressions shape whether they remain open to coaching in the future.

When leaders approach with visible, intentional respect, they earn something more powerful than authority—they earn permission to influence. Because when coaching feels like dignity, not discipline, it becomes something people welcome, not something they brace for. Blame, on the other hand, shuts people down. Curiosity opens them up. In the workplace, when something goes wrong, the instinct is often to assign blame: *Who skipped the check? Who didn't speak up? Who missed the cue?* But while this may resemble accountability, it rarely fosters learning. Instead, it creates silence, defensiveness, and a culture of avoidance—none of which support performance growth.

That's why real coaches use curiosity as a discipline.

When something breaks down—whether it's a process, a behaviour, or a decision—you don't start with "who messed up?" You start with:

>"What was happening around that moment?"
>"What were you seeing or interpreting?"
>"What made that option feel right at the time?"

This isn't letting people off the hook. It's **getting to the right hook**. Because if you skip straight to correction, you might fix the symptom while leaving the root untouched.

Take, for example, a worker who bypassed a lockout step. The easy response is to reprimand: "You missed a critical safety procedure—this is unacceptable."
But a coach will pause and ask:

>"What was your understanding of the step at that point?"
>"Had that procedure changed recently?"
>"Was there pressure to move faster on this shift?"

This line of questioning might reveal an overlooked comms update. Or an environment where safety corners get cut quietly to meet targets. Or it might reveal a mindset of assumption: "I've done this a hundred times—it felt safe."

Now you have something worth coaching. Not just the action—but the belief behind it.

This is the heart of no-blame conversations. They **prioritise insight over impulse**. They don't excuse mistakes—they explore them. And in doing so, they teach your team that feedback is a tool for growth, not a weapon for shame. But this only works if your tone backs up your words. You can't ask curious questions with a clenched jaw. You can't say "just trying to understand" while clearly waiting to pounce. Curiosity must be real—and that means leading the conversation without preloading the verdict.

You also need to **watch your timing**. Don't drag someone into a post-task review and launch into questions the moment they arrive. Let the dust settle. Let dignity reset. Then say:

> "Let's walk through it together. I want to understand what was guiding your decision there."

That simple phrase—*walk through it together*—shifts the power dynamic. It signals, *"I'm here with you, not above you. Let's learn from this, not run from it."* When leaders foster a no-blame coaching environment, people stop hiding and start sharing. They become more open about what they saw, what they feared, and where they need support. And that honesty is the real gold in coaching—it reveals what process metrics and safety reports never will. Blame creates caution. Curiosity builds capability. Abstract standards alone don't change behaviour; real-world consequences do. When coaching is framed with empathy and inquiry, it moves beyond compliance—it starts to grow competence.

You can remind someone of the procedure. You can point to the work instruction. But if they don't feel the reality of what's at stake, the standard becomes just another rule to follow when convenient. That's why great coaches don't stop at "what should be done"—they connect it to why it matters in the real world.

This is what we call using **resonating references**: anchoring accountability in lived, relatable risk—not theory, not policy, but something the person can see, remember, or feel.

It sounds like this:

> "This same step was missed on another site six months ago. That worker ended up with a torn shoulder. Not because they didn't care—but because the check wasn't reinforced."
> Or:
> "That shortcut might save 30 seconds today. But we've seen how it turns into 30 minutes of incident investigation when it compounds."

When you coach using resonant references, you shift the standard from something abstract to something deeply felt. You move from being perceived as a policy enforcer to being seen as a protector of belief. This approach is especially powerful when coaching newer workers who may have good intent but limited exposure to the risks involved in their tasks. Their technical understanding is still developing, and their sense of consequence is not yet fully formed. By anchoring your coaching in something real—a recent event, a past incident, or a field-level observation—you give them something memorable. It becomes a reference point they will recall the next time they face a similar situation. The key, however, is to maintain balance. The aim is not to scare people into compliance but to build care through context. So don't only reference what went wrong; reinforce what went right, too. This dual approach cultivates awareness without creating fear—and that's where real learning takes root. For example :

> "You know why that step mattered? Because it meant you spotted the tension in the cable before someone walked through it. That's how you prevented a near miss. That's what good coaching looks like in action."

This technique works even better when you reference their own previous performance. Nothing lands like a comparison to a moment they were proud of.

> "This isn't like how you handled that shift last week—you were sharp that day. I know what you're capable of. That's the level we're holding here."

Now you've done three things:

1. Reinforced belief in their capacity.

2. Anchored your feedback in a known, credible moment.

3. Made the coaching personal, not generic.

This is what makes a reference resonate—not that it sounds important, but that it feels real to them. Because standards don't live on paper. They live in memory, emotion, and consequence. And the more real you make those connections, the stronger the accountability becomes. Great coaches don't just correct—they notice. And what they choose to notice first sets the tone for everything that follows.

When you open a conversation by recognising what was done well, you're not softening the blow of feedback. You're reinforcing belief. You're telling the person, "I see your effort. I saw what you did well. Let's build on that." This matters, especially in environments where high standards meet high pressure.

Coaching that starts with recognition creates psychological safety. It says: "You're not in trouble—you're in development." That one shift in tone changes how people listen, how they reflect, and how they respond. Let's say a crew just completed a critical lift. You observed the task and noticed three things:

- The signal person maintained great eye contact.

- The team paused during a gust of wind without needing a prompt.

- But they missed one final check before unhooking.

You could jump straight to the missed check. And they'd brace for it. But if you lead with:

> "The way you paused during the wind shift—
> that showed judgement. And your eye signals
> were tight—clear, confident. Let's walk
> through that final check though. What
> happened there?"

Now you've reinforced their belief before asking them to correct something. You've protected their **sense of competence**, which makes them more willing to learn.

This isn't about sugar-coating mistakes. It's about **anchoring feedback in a full picture of performance**, not just the flaws. And it works even better when recognition is **specific**. Vague praise like "good job" doesn't reinforce anything. But when you say:

> "Your briefing before the task helped everyone know what to expect—that's what kept the setup calm,"

You're reinforcing a behaviour they can repeat. That's what recognition is for—not just to feel good, but to drive consistency. Celebration also plays a long game. When leaders consistently point out what's going well—not just what's missing—they shape the team's identity. Over time, people begin to take pride in the things that get recognised. They aim for standards not out of fear, but because it feels good to be seen doing something well. And there's another benefit: when it's time to give tough feedback, it lands better. Because your coaching track record says, "I don't just call you out—I call you up."

In short, recognition is not a reward—it is reinforcement. It is not something separate from coaching; it is the very beginning of it. Recognition signals what matters. It tells the person, *"This is what we value—do more of it."* So before you ask, correct, or challenge, pause and ask yourself: *What is one thing they did today that deserves to be reinforced?* Then start there. Because when you begin with belief, behaviour follows. Recognition sets the tone. It opens the door. And it lays the foundation for coaching to land where it matters most.

The difference between a strong correction and a damaging one often comes down to one word: **focus**. When leaders focus on facts—what was seen, what was done, and what standard it connects to—the conversation stays clear, actionable, and emotionally safe. But when correction slips into personality or vague judgement, it stops being helpful and starts eroding trust. Fact-based correction is a core leadership habit because it protects both **the person's dignity** and **the standard's integrity**.

Let's say someone bypassed a sign-off step on a confined space entry. You don't need to say:

> "You're careless,"
> or
> "You don't take things seriously."

Those are character attacks. And once you make it personal, you activate defence. The person stops listening and starts protecting. They won't reflect on the behaviour—they'll argue the identity.

Now contrast that with:

> "I observed that the sign-off wasn't completed before entry. That's a critical step in the confined space procedure. Walk me through what was happening at that point."

Now the focus is on the **action**, not the person. You've named what was seen, referenced the standard, and opened a window for dialogue. That's how coaching earns its power—not by accusation, but by observation.

The key to this approach is precision. Don't generalise with:

> "You're always rushing,"
> or
> "You're not paying attention lately."

Instead, say:

> "On this task, I noticed the checklist was skipped in the last two steps. What influenced that decision?"

You're keeping it **situational and specific**. You're coaching what happened, not who they are. And this precision also protects your credibility as a coach. When your feedback is based on what you saw—not what you feel or assume—it holds more weight. The team may not always agree with your interpretation, but they can't deny that you were present, observant, and fair

Fact-based correction also models what you want from your team: clear thinking under pressure. If you want them to reflect on actions and consequences, you have to do the same. Emotional corrections teach emotional responses. Clear corrections teach discipline, ownership, and maturity.

This approach works in both directions. When people experience your feedback as grounded in fact rather than emotion, they become more willing to surface issues early. They trust that the conversation won't spiral into blame or labels. That trust opens up the feedback loop and strengthens the leadership system. So the next time you step into a tough conversation, remember your role: you are not there to judge the person—you are there to help realign behaviour with the standard. And you do that with clarity, not character critiques. That is how you coach people toward improvement without damaging who they are. The moment your coaching starts sounding like a parent scolding a child, the learning stops.

Frontline coaching isn't about asserting rank. It's about raising capability. And the most effective way to do that is to coach **adult to adult**—with mutual respect, shared responsibility, and clear expectations. Because when you speak to someone as a peer in ownership, you invite them to rise to the standard—not shrink under it.[10]

This doesn't mean pretending hierarchy doesn't exist. As a leader, you do hold authority. But great coaches don't lean on authority as a crutch. They lean on **influence, presence, and credibility**. That's what makes adult-to-adult dialogue powerful. It assumes that the other person has the capacity to self-correct, to think, and to grow.

It sounds like:

> "Let's step through this together and see what we might need to adjust."
> Or:
> "I trust your judgement—what's your read on what happened here?"

That language sends a signal:

> "You're capable. You're accountable. I'm not here to police you—I'm here to partner with you to get it right."

Adult-to-adult coaching also means being direct without being demeaning. It means naming what matters, clearly:

> "This isn't aligned with our agreed standard. I know you care about doing it right. Let's reset that together."

You're not sugar-coating. But you're also not humiliating. You're holding the line and holding belief. This approach is especially critical in moments of friction—when the behaviour is clearly off, or the person is frustrated, disengaged, or under pressure. If you drop into a top-down, punitive tone, you reinforce fear. But if you maintain adult posture—steady, composed, and clear—you model the same maturity you want reflected back. It also works in reverse. If the person reacts defensively, becomes emotional, or tries to offload accountability, an adult-to-adult frame lets you say:

"I'm here to work with you, not against you. Let's focus on what we can adjust and move forward with."

This approach to coaching de-escalates tension, redirects focus, and reinforces partnership—without ever lowering the standard. Beneath this method lies a deeper truth: adult-to-adult dialogue creates a culture where ownership becomes the norm. People begin to expect respectful, direct conversations. They arrive ready to answer for decisions, to reflect on outcomes, and to engage constructively. And over time, they pass that same tone to others. What leaders model is what teams mirror. When coaching remains grounded in mutual respect and adult-level accountability, it reshapes the culture. Conversations become more open. Accountability feels safer. And the standard is maintained not because it is enforced, but because it is owned. That is what sustainable leadership sounds like. But coaching is not complete until it results in a clear next step. Even the best conversation loses its impact if it ends with a vague promise, a polite nod, or an unspoken assumption.

That's why great coaches close every session with **a visible agreement**—an action, a commitment, or a change that's understood by both sides. Because clarity creates accountability. And vagueness, no matter how well-intended, creates drift.

Let's be honest—most coaching that doesn't stick fails at the close. You talk through the issue, gain alignment, maybe even hit some good insights. But then it ends with:

> "Okay, just keep that in mind next time."
> or
> "Let's try to be more aware going forward."

There's nothing wrong with the intent. But without something to track, reflect on, or verify, it stays abstract. The learning fades. The moment passes. Instead, leaders should always guide toward a **simple, specific outcome**. Something like:

> "Before next shift, write down the three cues you'll use to trigger that safety check."
> "Let's make the first 10 minutes of tomorrow's toolbox talk about how we'll reinforce this across the crew."
> "Next week, I want to hear how you handled this with your peer. What's your plan?"

These aren't punishments—they're **coaching loops**. They let the person move from awareness to action, and they give the leader a legitimate point of follow-up that isn't micromanagement—it's development.

The goal isn't to create more admin. The goal is to **build follow-through into your leadership habit**.

That means:

- Make it visible. Write it on a card, say it aloud, recap it clearly.

- Make it actionable. Tie it to a task, a standard, a shift, or a behaviour.

- Make it shared. Both coach and coachee should know what's agreed and why.

This is especially important when there's been a gap in performance. Accountability without clarity is just pressure. But accountability with a shared agreement becomes **empowering**. The person knows what success looks like. They know what they're working toward. And they know you'll be checking in—not to catch them out, but to confirm growth.

The ripple effect: when teams get used to coaching that ends in clear action, they start self-correcting faster. They anticipate the check-in. They initiate the follow-up. They build self-leadership inside your system.

Because the expectation is no longer just, "Do better." It's:

"Here's the next step we both agree will move this forward."

And when that agreement is kept, belief grows—not just in the system, but in the individual. They begin to trust their own judgment, their ability to follow through, and their role in upholding the standard. Coaching isn't only about what gets corrected. It's just as much about what gets strengthened. Each conversation is a chance to reinforce confidence, clarify expectations, and build momentum—not just fix mistakes.

If a person walks away from a coaching session with only instructions, you've managed the task. But if they walk away with a clearer understanding of the why, the how, and the principles behind the task, you've built competence. That's the mark of real coaching—**not just compliance, but uplift**.

Too many coaching conversations are focused on the error. The gap. The issue. But if that's where the dialogue ends, all you've done is highlight a problem. Coaching that uplifts does more. It helps the person see what they can now do that they couldn't see before. It raises the ceiling of their performance, not just repositions the floor.

This is where coaching shifts from corrective to developmental.

> "Let's walk through what you now understand differently."
> "If someone else were struggling with this, how would you coach them through it?"
> "What did you learn about your decision-making under pressure today?"

These questions aren't just post-mortem reflections—they're tools to **surface capability**. And once a person says their insight aloud, it becomes part of their operating system. It becomes repeatable.

Here's the difference:

- **Instruction** tells them what to do next time.

- **Uplift** teaches them how to think better every time.

And the benefit compounds. When people consistently walk away from coaching with stronger judgement, sharper awareness, and clearer standards, they don't just avoid repeating errors—they build momentum. They become safer, smarter, and more proactive.

You'll notice it in how they talk:

> "I was about to rush, but I remembered what we said about cueing off the site lead's position."
> Or:
> "This step used to trip me up, but now I anchor it to the checklist point—it's embedded."

That's not accident. That's uplift. That's what coaching done well leaves behind.

It also signals to your team that your coaching isn't just for correction—it's a path to **growth**. People begin to seek it out. They start to ask, "Can we run through that together?" not because they're unsure, but because they've learned that coaching sharpens them. That's the culture you're building. So don't just end a session with a recap. End it with a step forward in competence. Make that the measure of success: Did this person leave better equipped than they arrived? Because that's the real work of leadership: Not managing performance, but multiplying capability.

Chapter 8:

Development Is a Team Sport

Coaching doesn't live in theory. It lives inside pressure.

In any real operating environment, leaders aren't coaching in a blank space—they're coaching under constraints. Shifts must be delivered. Targets must be met. Downtime must be avoided. The question isn't "Should we coach?" It's "How do we coach inside the noise without losing the point?"

That's why the first step in any sustainable coaching approach is to **accept the conditions as they are**. Not idealised. Not softened. But real. And then to connect your capability development efforts directly to the demands of the work. In other words: coaching must align with delivery.

If you're coaching skills that don't connect to immediate outputs, the team will nod, agree—and forget. Not because they don't care. But because the coaching feels **disconnected from what success actually looks like today**. That's when coaching becomes background noise—well-intentioned, but ignored.

Instead, your coaching has to speak the language of production:

> "How does this skill improve the flow of this task?"
> "How does this behaviour reduce rework or safety exposure under pressure?"
> "How does reinforcing this step make us more resilient when things go wrong?"

The moment your coaching begins to answer those questions, it gains immediate relevance. The team stops viewing it as something separate from performance and starts recognising it as a support mechanism for delivering results. To achieve that, you must stay in touch with the current operational context—the pressure profile the crew is navigating. Are they short-staffed? Behind on schedule? Struggling with poor handover data? If your coaching does not acknowledge that reality, it risks sounding naive—or worse, disconnected. But when you do acknowledge it, something shifts. A message like, *"I know this week we're stretched on man-hours. That's why I want to coach task clarity—so we don't waste motion or make rework errors,"* lands with weight. It resonates because it links the coaching focus directly to what the team is managing in real time. That is how coaching becomes practical, purposeful, and welcomed.

This is not about lowering the bar—it is about choosing the right bar for the current conditions and then coaching for strength within those boundaries. That is what makes capability development durable—not just aspirational. Before coaching the individual, first scan the system they are performing in. Pay attention to shift rhythm, delivery demands, cross-functional tension, handover stability, and task setup. Then ask yourself: *What capability matters most in this context? What specific behaviour will improve performance here, today?* Coaching in the vacuum of theory may feel effective on paper, but coaching in alignment with operational context is what keeps standards real and actionable. That is how leaders maintain high expectations without losing relevance.

Every coaching moment happens inside a triangle—whether you name it or not. On one side is **People**: skills, beliefs, motivation, and teamwork. On the second is **Production**: shift targets, technical delivery, and time pressure. On the third is **Conditions**: the environment, systems, structure, tools, and constraints.

This triangle is your coaching reality. And if you don't account for all three sides, your coaching becomes unbalanced. You might reinforce the right behaviours but under the wrong pressure. You might diagnose skill gaps without seeing the system frictions that cause them. Or worse—you might coach effort when the problem is structural. Studies in human factors and operational reliability show that coaching is most effective when it considers all three system forces—people, process, and context—rather than focusing on individual performance in isolation. This triadic lens helps leaders address root causes, not just surface behaviour [11].

That's why the best coaches read the whole triangle before acting.

Let's take an example. A new crew is consistently missing its inspection handover target. On the surface, it looks like a **People** issue—lack of discipline or awareness. But look closer: the shift lead hasn't been trained in the updated checklist (**People**), the schedule leaves no clean window for pre-checks (**Production**), and the toolbox is missing two critical instruments (**Conditions**).If you only coach one side, you'll misfire. You'll give performance feedback to someone who doesn't have the setup. Or you'll push productivity without reinforcing capability. Either way, belief erodes—and outcomes stall.

That's why the triangle matters. It helps you ask the right leadership questions before jumping in:

- **People** – Do they have the skill, belief, and shared understanding to do this well?

- **Production** – Are current delivery expectations realistic and well-sequenced?

- **Conditions** – Are the systems and setups helping or hindering the outcome?

Every coaching conversation should include a quiet mental scan of that triangle. You don't need a checklist—you need awareness.

Because here's what happens when you get it right:

- Your coaching gets sharper. You're not guessing—you're diagnosing.

- Your team gets safer. They trust that your feedback isn't detached—it's grounded in their actual experience.

- Your system gets stronger. You stop patching problems and start reinforcing **conditions that support performance**.

Coaching without this context becomes personal. Coaching **with** it becomes practical, strategic, and fair.

So the next time you step into a conversation, pause. Ask yourself:

> "Which side of the triangle is this issue really sitting on?"
> And then coach from that side, with full visibility of the others.

That's how leaders turn coaching from opinion into operating strength.

Every workplace has its own rhythm. Every team has its own pressure profile. And every leader must learn how to coach **within** that reality—not outside it.

You can't copy-and-paste a coaching script from one location to another and expect it to land. What works on a stable, well-sequenced production line might fall flat in a high-variability shutdown. What resonates with a mature crew might confuse a new hire team still finding their footing. That's why effective coaches take time to **read the terrain**. Before they correct, they observe. Before they reinforce, they calibrate. Because coaching without adaptation isn't leadership—it's theatre. It might sound good, but it won't change anything.

Let's say you've just joined a new site. You walk into a team where the structures are loose, shift handovers are messy, and most routines rely on experience rather than formal checks. If you try to introduce a complex coaching cadence right away, you'll overwhelm the system. You'll get polite compliance—or silent pushback.

But if you start by tightening one visible routine—like task briefings—and coach within that routine, your message will land. You're adapting to the environment, not fighting it. And the team sees that you're serious about both performance and relevance. This doesn't mean you lower standards. It means you build capability **in a sequence that fits the system's current strength**. You ask:

- What routines are already present and respected?

- Where is belief strongest—and where is it fragile?

- What's the crew's current tolerance for change?

When you have that insight, you don't waste effort on misplaced coaching. You apply your energy where the system is ready to grow—and you let that growth build credibility for the next layer. It's also important to note: your **own leadership rhythm** must adapt too. Don't overload yourself trying to hit every touchpoint at once. Start where traction is possible, build early wins, and scale from there. In a constrained environment, your consistency is more powerful than your coverage.

Adapting your coaching does not mean becoming reactive; it means remaining strategic, even when flexibility is necessary. You can still uphold standards, reinforce expectations, and build belief—but you do so with situational awareness and context sensitivity. The most powerful coaching is not the most polished or perfectly scripted—it is the coaching that is well-placed, well-timed, and well-aligned with how your team actually operates. That is how coaching becomes integrated into the system, rather than feeling like noise layered on top of it. Leadership loses its effectiveness the further it drifts from the work. That is why the most credible, impactful coaching happens at the coalface—close to the task, alongside the crew, and within the real-world noise of daily delivery. Leaders who remain close to where the work happens do not just coach better—they lead better.

Proximity gives you insight. You see decisions in context. You notice friction in the workflow before it turns into failure. You hear the way people speak to each other, watch how standards are interpreted, and sense whether belief is rising or fading. But proximity isn't just about being physically present. It's about **being tuned in**, available, and engaged without hovering. Your goal isn't to manage every step—it's to **stay close enough to influence what matters, while giving space for ownership to grow.**

This is where many leaders get it wrong. They either withdraw into the office—only showing up when there's an issue—or they overcompensate and start micromanaging. Neither approach creates a coaching culture. One builds detachment. The other builds dependence.

Field-based leadership hits the balance. It says:

> "I'm here often enough to know what's real."
> "I'm present enough to notice growth or drift before reports tell me."
> "I coach from what I see, not just what I hear."

Proximity also sharpens your coaching questions. When you're close to the task, you can ask:

> "Why did we choose that order of steps?"
> "What was the plan going in—and what changed?"
> "How did that adjustment affect the pace or the risk?"

These moments are not theoretical. They are grounded in what you just observed—which is precisely why they land with impact. For the crew, proximity changes perception.

You are no longer a distant figure reviewing charts from afar; you are the leader who walks the floor, sees the work, and still has something valuable to say—not just about targets, but about technique, rhythm, and team habits. This kind of leadership builds trust—and it sharpens timing. It helps you sense when to intervene and when to step back, when someone needs reinforcement and when they are ready to stretch. That level of insight cannot be found in dashboards; it comes from presence. And ultimately, proximity reinforces belief. When you coach at the coalface, your presence communicates one powerful message: I see you, I believe in your potential, and your development matters. Your presence says:

> "This work matters. I'm not above it. I'm part of shaping it."

That message is powerful. Because in high-demand environments, people don't just need direction—they need to know their effort is seen, understood, and developed in real time.

That is the true gift of coalface leadership—not control, and not visibility, but credibility earned through proximity. It comes from being close enough to coach what truly counts. Coaching is one of the most powerful leadership assets you have—but it only delivers value when it is invested where it creates traction. In most work environments, leaders cannot afford to coach everything at once. Time is limited. Presence is finite. Emotional bandwidth must be managed carefully. That is why you need a practical tool to help you decide: Where will my coaching effort have the greatest impact—on both delivery and belief?

That's the purpose of the **Leadership Leverage Triangle**. It's a practical lens that helps you align your coaching priorities with what the business actually needs from your team.

The triangle consists of three coaching leverage points:

1. **Capability** – Do they have the skills, habits, and understanding to deliver the task consistently

under pressure?

2. **Belief** – Do they see the task as important? Do they believe their role matters in delivering it right?

3. **Conditions** – Are the systems, routines, and structures enabling the task—or making it harder than it needs to be?

A strategic leadership model to illustrate the dynamic relationship between people capability, business outcomes, and the operating conditions that connect and influence both. The triangle equips leaders to apply coaching and leadership practices in a way that is grounded in real-world context—aligning development efforts with operational demands and performance expectations.

Each point of the triangle affects performance. But you can't coach them all at once. Your job is to assess: Which of these is breaking first? And then direct your energy **where it will release the most performance tension**.

Let's say a team is consistently falling behind on routine inspections. If you jump straight to skills coaching, you might run training that doesn't solve the real issue. But if you pause and scan the triangle, you might realise:

- The process is known (**Capability**)

- But belief is low—people see the inspection as admin, not value (**Belief**)

- And the form is clunky, with no time allowance in the shift structure (**Conditions**)

Now your leverage point is clear. You need to coach belief while surfacing a system constraint. Your coaching might sound like:

> "Let's revisit why this check matters—not just for compliance, but for avoiding rework."
>
> "And let's look at how we're structuring time to do it properly."

This is what it means to coach with leverage. You are not simply reacting to problems—you are diagnosing root causes. You are not pushing harder—you are coaching smarter. The Leadership Leverage Triangle™ helps you avoid burnout by showing you where to focus. When leaders consistently pour coaching energy into building individual capability while belief is eroding or systems are misaligned, they begin to fatigue—and so does the team.

But when coaching aligns with what the moment truly needs, it generates traction, not resistance. This requires a shift in mindset: from asking, *"What should I say here?"* to asking, *"What part of this triangle needs my focus?"* When applied consistently, the Leadership Leverage Triangle™ helps you build not just isolated coaching conversations, but an integrated coaching system. You begin to see how performance, belief, and structure interact—and you use that insight to lead with precision. Because real leadership is not about being everywhere. It is about knowing exactly where to apply your effort—and why. Before you coach the crew, scan the system they're operating in. That is how leveraged leadership begins. That's the mindset behind **monitor and diagnose**—a frontline leader's ability to assess the actual conditions, patterns, and readiness levels of their team without relying on reports or assumptions. It's not about audits. It's about sharp, repeatable observation that informs where and how you coach.

Think of monitoring as a simple question you carry everywhere:

> "Is this team set up to succeed today—or are we coaching on top of chaos?"

Many coaching efforts fail not because the message is wrong, but because the context is misread. You reinforce standards when the real issue is sequencing. You challenge behaviour when the tools are broken. You push mindset when the shift plan is stacked against them. That's why strong leaders diagnose before they coach. They use their walk-throughs, conversations, and pre-task observations to quietly gather answers to practical questions like:

- Are roles clearly understood within the task team?

- Is today's production plan realistic and well-communicated?

- What's the mood? Are people present, distracted, engaged?

- Are the right tools and checklists available—and being used?

- Is belief in the process visible—or just compliance?

These aren't formal metrics. They're **field-level indicators**. And over time, they give you a sense of your team's health. You'll start noticing which teams need skill-based coaching, which need reinforcement of belief, and which simply need help fixing the clutter in their setup.

Here's the key: local diagnostics must be **frequent, fast, and frictionless**. Don't wait for something to break before you assess. Make it part of your habit.

For example:

- A three-minute scan of a toolbox talk tells you more about culture than a full survey.

- Watching one routine task—without interruption—gives you better data than a report summary.

Listening to the way team members close out a job reveals how much ownership is in play.

And once you've got your read, your coaching becomes sharper. You're not guessing. You're not hoping it sticks. You're applying leadership energy where it will land and grow. This is where system leadership meets tactical coaching. You're building a real-time feedback loop—not just for individuals, but for the conditions that shape them. Because when you run diagnostics before giving direction, you coach with **context, confidence, and credibility**. And your team can feel the difference

If you only coach outcomes, you're always reacting.
If you coach the process, you shape what happens before it breaks.

The difference between reactive leadership and systems coaching often comes down to this one habit: the ability to see **flow**—how work actually moves through the system—and to notice where it gets stuck. This is where upstream coaching begins.

Instead of waiting until the end of shift to debrief what went wrong, great coaches walk the process. They ask:

- "Where does this task usually slow down?"

- "Which step gets skipped when we're under pressure?"

- "What decisions are people making earlier that shape the outcome later?"

This is called **coaching upstream**—catching the belief, behaviour, or setup before the visible failure point. And it starts by mapping the task flow—not in theory, but in the real-world version your team lives.

For example:
A recurring maintenance delay might look like a technician issue on the surface. But if you trace it upstream, you might find:

- The handover from ops was rushed.

- The isolation form wasn't prepped.

- The starter kit was missing key tools.

So while the fix is happening at Step 6, the coaching needs to happen at Step 2.

This mindset is what separates busy leaders from effective ones. It's not about reacting faster. It's about **seeing earlier**.
And the more fluent you become in process flow, the more strategic your coaching becomes.

Here's how to build that habit:

1. **Walk the task forward.** Observe how people prepare, sequence, and execute—not just how they finish.

2. **Ask backward-looking questions early.** At task start-up, ask: "What are you watching out for this time?" or "Where did this go off-track last time?"

3. **Surface pain points gently.** Don't interrogate—investigate: "If we had to improve this by 10%, where would you start?"

4. **Watch for workaround patterns.** If the same step is always skipped, adjusted, or rushed, it's not a one-off—it's a signal.

When you coach upstream, you're no longer just chasing quality or safety. You're coaching **how belief and behaviour show up in flow**—and that makes every improvement stick deeper. It also gives your team a new way to think. They stop waiting to be corrected. They start

anticipating where their choices shape the outcome. That's how process awareness becomes part of the culture. Because good teams deliver. Great teams deliver and diagnose. And that only happens when leaders show them how to read the process—not just survive it.

Coaching without diagnosing the system is like planting seeds in concrete. You might get effort—but you won't get growth.

That's why one of the most important leadership habits in constrained environments is learning to **scan for enablers and barriers**. These are the unseen forces that make or break daily delivery—and they either reinforce or sabotage your coaching efforts.

Let's start with enablers. These are the structures, tools, behaviours, and rhythms that support performance:

- A clear shift plan that gives enough time for quality execution.

- A checklist that prompts critical decisions in the right order.

- A team member who models the standard and influences others.

- A routine coaching window where reflection is expected and safe.

When you spot an enabler, reinforce it.
Name it. Praise it. Embed it deeper.

> "The way you ran that toolbox talk—it set the tone. That's an enabler for the whole shift."

> "This board layout makes progress visible—let's protect that as a non-negotiable."

Now on the other side: **barriers**. These are the constraints, friction points, gaps, or habits that trip the team—no matter how skilled or motivated they are:

- A misaligned production target that pressures people to cut corners.

- A poorly sequenced task that creates confusion mid-job.

- A missing tool, a broken printer, or a form no one understands.

- A culture where only problems get attention, but effort doesn't.

When you see these, don't coach around them. Coach into them.
Name the barrier clearly. Ask the crew how it's showing up. Bring it to the surface so it can be addressed—either by your team, your coaching, or the broader system.

This is critical: coaching doesn't replace system correction.

But it does help reveal where system correction is needed.

You might say:

> "I've seen this step get skipped three times this week. Is the sequence realistic for how your day is actually structured?"
> Or:
> "I notice we're rushing pre-start checks— what's making that difficult to do properly right now?"

These aren't complaints. They're **coaching diagnostics**.

And over time, they help your team learn to surface issues themselves. Instead of normalising friction, they learn to flag it. Instead of working around barriers, they become participants in removing them. And when that happens, your coaching begins to scale. It's no longer dependent on your presence. It becomes embedded in how the team thinks, plans, and performs.

So make this your quiet discipline:

> Every time you see a performance issue, ask:
>
> "Is there an enabler we're not using—or a barrier we haven't addressed?"

That single question can turn a frustrated leader into a systems coach.
And it can turn a stuck team into a high-performing one.

PART 3:

DESIGN WHAT GOOD LOOKS LIKE

Chapter 9:

A Playbook That Actually Works

In the realm of transformative coaching, we explore a coaching technique that synergises creative coaching elements with a robust scientific basis. It integrates creativity and empirical methods, revolutionising frontline leadership coaching with a blend of intuitive understanding and methodical strategies.

This is a powerful tool that combines scientific principles and psychological insights to guide individuals through self-reflection and critical thinking. At the heart of the concept of metacognition, which involves being aware of and evaluating one's own thought processes. This self-reflection allows individuals to analyse their decisions and behaviours and understand their impacts on both the team and the organisation. By fostering this awareness, this helps individuals to gain a deeper understanding of their actions and motivations, promoting personal growth and effective leadership.[12]

Reflective practices are closely linked to emotional intelligence, a concept popularised by Daniel Goleman [13]. Emotional intelligence involves understanding one's emotions and their influence on behaviour, which is crucial for navigating complex interpersonal dynamics and enhancing one's capacity for self-improvement. Through reflective practices, individuals can better manage their emotions and develop stronger interpersonal relationships, contributing to a more cohesive and effective team.

The model also draws on the Socratic method, using probing questions to stimulate critical thinking and self-reflection[14]. This approach encourages individuals to examine their thoughts and behaviours more deeply, leading to a clearer understanding of their actions and motivations. By inviting individuals to reflect on their experiences, it supports cognitive restructuring—the process of identifying and changing unhelpful thinking patterns and behaviours. This, in turn, fosters lasting behavioural change and continuous personal growth.

At its core, the approach creates a supportive environment where individuals feel safe exploring their thoughts and emotions. Through thoughtful, open-ended questioning, it guides people to uncover their own insights, cultivating a sense of ownership over their development. The process promotes growth, builds personal responsibility, and offers a balanced, reflective coaching experience.

By integrating metacognition, emotional intelligence, and the Socratic method, it offers a well-rounded and practical path toward self-discovery and continuous improvement

Reflective Coaching Loop

A practical coaching model illustrating the internal process of guided self-awareness that leads to behavioural shift.

The loop equips leaders to engage others through presence, curiosity, and insight—creating space for individuals to observe, explore, reflect, and reframe. It supports transformational growth by aligning coaching conversations with the deeper human dynamics that shape action, mindset, and adaptation.

The coaching questions used in this approach are intentionally crafted to foster self-reflection and awareness, helping individuals recognise their performance patterns, challenges, and areas for growth. For each key dimension, a variety of alternative questions are offered—each with a distinct purpose and context—to support both the coach and the individual throughout their development journey.

This chapter outlines a practical blueprint for applying a reflective coaching approach that helps leaders and teams move through meaningful transformation. At its heart is the art of asking the right questions—questions that unlock self-awareness, encourage growth, and lead to lasting improvement.

1. Self-Reflection: "Reflect"

Key Question: "How do you think you went with that?"

• Aligned Questions:

1. "Can you describe your experience during this task?"

2. "What are your thoughts on how the process unfolded?"

3. "In your view, how effectively did you handle the task?"

Intent: These questions initiate the reflective process, encouraging coachees to introspect on their performance and experiences, laying the groundwork for deeper understanding and self-awareness.

2. Celebrate Success: "Achieve"

Key Question: "What do you think you did well?"

• Aligned Questions:

1. "What aspects of the task do you feel most proud of?"

2. "Can you identify any strengths you displayed during this activity?"

3. "What parts of the task do you think went smoothly and why?"

Intent: These questions highlight the positive aspects, allowing coachees to recognise and articulate their strengths and successful components of their performance, fostering a sense of achievement and motivation.

3. Opportunity Identification: "Discover"

Key Question: "What do you think you did not do well?"

• Aligned Questions:

1. "Were there any parts of the task that you found challenging?"

2. "In hindsight, what would you do differently?"

3. "Can you think of any areas where you feel you could have performed better?"

Intent: Focusing on areas for improvement, these questions guide coachees to identify opportunities for growth, setting the stage for development and skill enhancement.

4. Impact Exploration: "Impact"

Key Question: "What do you think are the consequences of that?"

•Aligned Questions:

1. "How do you think your performance affected the overall outcome?"

2. "What do you believe are the implications of the challenges you faced?"

3. "In what ways do you think your approach impacted the task and others involved?"

Intent: These questions encourage coachees to consider the broader implications of their actions, deepening their understanding of the impact and consequences of their performance.

5. Action Commitment: "Commit"

Key Question: What one action will you take to turn today's insight into progress?

• Aligned Questions:

1. Based on our conversation, what's one thing you will intentionally do differently next time?

2. What's one behaviour you'll shift to influence a better result next time?

3. What specific action will you take to address the challenge we talked about?

Intent: Encouraging proactive thinking about personal development, these questions help coachee's set clear goals for improvement, culminating in a commitment to action and continuous growth.

By utilising these structured coaching questions, leaders can guide their teams through a journey of self-discovery and learning. This process not only enhances individual capabilities but also aligns behaviours with organisational goals and standards, fostering an environment of continuous improvement and development.

The core intent behind these questions is to guide the coachee through a process of self-discovery and learning, enabling them to assess their performance and critically identify areas for growth. This approach helps develop their capabilities and align their behaviour with expected standards and goals. Through these questions, the coach facilitates a supportive environment where the coachee can openly reflect and plan for future development.

Reflective mirroring, rooted in psychological principles, is a key aspect of this approach. Coaches listen attentively and reflect the coachee's innermost thoughts and emotions, facilitating deeper self-understanding and personal growth. This technique goes beyond surface-level awareness, enabling individuals to overcome perceived limitations and uncover deeper truths about themselves, fostering significant personal development.

Coaching emphasises the importance of building trust through active listening and empathetic feedback, following psychological research that highlights these elements as crucial for effective communication. This approach not only strengthens interpersonal relationships but also enhances personal and professional skills essential for leadership and team cooperation. It facilitates a journey of self-discovery and empowerment, leading to stronger connections and empathetic leadership qualities.

Strategic questioning encourages in-depth self-exploration and perspective shifts. These questions are designed to challenge and stimulate new ways of thinking, leading coachee's to re-evaluate their approaches and foster personal growth and innovation. This method offers an expanded understanding and nuanced views on both personal and professional challenges.

Feedback derived from observations are shared clearly; the impact of actions is discussed; listening ensures an understanding of the coachee's perspective, and suggestions are offered for improvement. This comprehensive feedback mechanism is crucial in transforming coaching from mere observation to a process that actively contributes to the coachee's developmental journey.

Coaching with insights treats coaching as an art form, where coaches guide team members from a state of vague self-awareness to clearer, more impactful insights. This method is about carefully shaping a masterpiece, acknowledging the distinct qualities of each coachee, and aiding them in achieving their utmost potential.

Real-time coaching is marked by dynamic interaction, active listening, and responsive engagement. This approach emphasises immediate feedback, allowing coachee's to apply insights and adjust in real time, accelerating their personal and professional growth.

This innovative methodology not only inspires individual development but also drives organisational success, proving to be an indispensable tool in today's dynamic business world. It represents a significant advancement in the realms of coaching and leadership development, promoting growth and excellence at both individual and organisational levels.

Case Studies

In theory, this is what a coaching session would look and feel like:

1. "Looking at the activity as a whole, **how do you feel** you did with that" (activity, meeting, facilitation, task execution)

2. "What do you **think you did well**?" Allow coachee to respond and if relevant then go to point 2.5 and if not proceed to point 3.

> 2.5 "**I observed that** you did do well on ...." (give positive feedback on observed behaviour meeting expectations or performance standard)

3. "What do you **think you did not do well**?" Allow coachee to respond and if relevant then go to 3.5 and if not proceed to point 4.

> 3.5 **I observed that you did not do well** on .... (If what the coachee raised on point 3 is not as important as your observation e.g. process, SOP or standard not followed or unsafe)

4. "**What is the consequence of** what you did not do well?"

"What is **your improvement action** for next time you conduct this activity"

The sequence of open-ended questions is critical to achieving meaningful outcomes—and should not be altered. Changing the order risks weakening the depth of self-reflection and, ultimately, the individual's commitment to change. The first three questions are carefully designed to build understanding and internalise the impact of behaviour. They guide the individual to reflect deeply on consequences, making the need for action feel real, relevant, and personal.

In practice this is what it would feel and sound like:

Scenario: You accompany a supervisor to conduct a safety interaction in the field where the team is setting up scaffolding to prepare for a working-at-height task due to be done today. You observe that a risk analysis is available, the team has the correct PPE, and a barricade has not been erected to deny access to the task execution area.

P1-Setting Expectations:

Leader: "Good morning, team. I see you have set up scaffolding to prepare for a working-at-height task scheduled for today. I'd like to have a quick safety interaction with you before you begin. Is it alright if we stop work for a moment to discuss your preparations?"

Team: "Sure, that's fine."

Leader: "Great. I can see you've set up the scaffolding and are ready to begin the task. How do you think you have done with preparations?"

Supervisor: "I think we did well. We made sure everyone had the correct PPE and reviewed the risk analysis before starting.

P2-Monitoring Performance:

Leader: "What do you think you have done well?"

Supervisor: We made sure everyone had the right PPE, reviewed the risk analysis, checked the equipment, verified the requested scaffold height, appointed a spotter, and clearly assigned tasks before starting

Leader: "Excellent job on those aspects. Consistent PPE use and thorough risk assessments are crucial for safety. What do you think you have not done well?"

P3-Coaching to Address Performance Gaps:

Supervisor: "We prepared well; I cannot see anything not done right."

Leader: "I noticed the barricade has not been set up yet. What do you think are the consequences of not having the barricade?"

Supervisor: "It increases the risk of unauthorised access and potential accidents."

Leader: "Absolutely. Not having the barricade could lead to serious safety issues. What potential accidents do you think could occur when the barricade is not in place?"

Supervisor: "They could trip over the equipment, or worse, be in the path of falling objects from the scaffolding."

Leader: "Exactly. And if an accident were to happen, what would be the implications for our team?"

Supervisor: "It would mean injuries, potential delays, and an investigation into the safety breach. It could have serious consequences, causing harm and serious injury to someone. One of us might not go back home the same after an injury."

Leader: "Right. So, ensuring that we have all safety controls in place, like the barricade, is not just a formality—it's crucial for preventing accidents and maintaining a safe work environment. What can we do right now to make it safer?"

Supervisor: "We will erect the barricade and put controls in place to prevent unauthorised access and potential accidents."

Leader: "What is your commitment for next time you conduct this activity?"

Supervisor: "When we conduct our safety risk analysis, we will mark the controls as done only after they have been properly implemented. This will ensure that all hazard controls are actually in place before we consider them completed."

Leader: "That sounds like a solid plan. Let's implement that and review it during our next safety interaction. Ensuring every step is followed will significantly improve our safety measures. Let's continue to have a safe day and thank you for your time today."

Why Reflective Coaching is Effective and Sustainable

This case study demonstrates the effectiveness and sustainability of this coaching approach through several key elements:

1. **Respectful Approach:**
   - The leader begins by respectfully asking for permission to discuss safety, setting a tone of mutual respect and collaboration.

2. **No Blame Policy:**
   - Instead of blaming the supervisor for the oversight, the leader focuses on understanding the process and finding ways to prevent similar errors in the future. This fosters a culture of continuous improvement rather than fear of punishment.

3. **Resonating References:**
   - By discussing the potentially life-altering consequences of not having the barricade, the leader helps the supervisor and team internalise the seriousness of safety protocols. This deepens their understanding and commitment to following them.

4. **Recognition and Celebration:**
   - The leader acknowledges and celebrates the aspects of the preparation that were done well,

reinforcing positive behaviours and boosting morale.

5. **Fact-Based Correction:**
   - The conversation is based on observable facts (the barricade was not set up), not personal attacks. This ensures the interaction is objective and constructive.

6. **Adult-to-Adult Conversation:**
   - The interaction is conducted as an adult-to-adult conversation, where both parties are treated with respect and expected to take responsibility for their actions.

7. **Focused Interaction:**
   - The discussion is focused on safety, a critical aspect of the task at hand, ensuring that the conversation is relevant and impactful.

8. **Clear Outcomes and Actions:**
   - The leader and supervisor agree on a clear plan to address the oversight, ensuring that corrective actions are understood and will be implemented.

9. **Competency Uplift:**
   - The supervisor leaves the conversation with a better understanding of the importance of each safety step and a commitment to self-correct in the future, demonstrating an uplift in competency and ownership.

Positive Impact on Coach and Coachee

- **Leader's Perspective:**
    - The leader adds value by ensuring safety protocols are followed and by fostering a positive and proactive safety culture.

- o This approach reinforces the leader's role as a guide and supporter, rather than an enforcer, building trust and respect within the team.
- **Coachee's Perspective:**
  - o The supervisor feels valued and appreciated for their efforts, while also recognising the importance of the corrective action.
  - o By internalising the consequences of the oversight, the supervisor is more likely to self-correct in the future, reducing the need for constant reminders from the leader.

Coaching transforms routine interactions into powerful opportunities for growth and improvement. It seamlessly blends evaluation and feedback with supportive and respectful dialogue, ensuring that the team not only meets but exceeds expectations. This method results in a more capable and engaged workforce, dedicated to continuous improvement, and stands as a testament to the power of effective leadership in fostering a thriving workplace culture.

A key aspect of this method is framing corrections as opportunities for growth rather than reprimands. This transforms potentially negative feedback into empowering experiences. The leader is perceived as a mentor and supporter, reinforcing a culture of mutual respect and teamwork. By maintaining a respectful, fact-based, and solution-oriented approach, the team feels valued and motivated to strive for excellence, resulting in a more competent, confident, and cohesive workforce dedicated to maintaining high standards.

Despite its evaluative nature, this approach to coaching does not feel like a burden, an audit, or an assessment, even though in many ways it encompasses all of these elements. Instead, it fosters a collaborative and supportive environment where the focus is on growth and improvement. This approach has earned me tremendous success and has proven to create a positive workplace environment where employees thrive and excel.

Clear communication of expectations, acknowledgment of good practices, and constructive handling of mistakes contribute to a sense of shared purpose and cohesion. Employees feel appreciated and are more likely to take proactive steps to improve their performance. The framework's incorporation of these wholesome elements catalyses successful coaching outcomes, making it an effective and sustainable approach to leadership and development

I am reminded of a coaching program lead who once said, "Even if someone else may have the same template or cue cards, if they don't know the nuances of using them effectively, they can't duplicate your successful results and coaching outcomes." (Thanks, JF). This highlights the importance of understanding and mastering the subtleties which goes beyond the mere tools and frameworks, emphasising the skillful and empathetic application of coaching principles. This mastery is what truly differentiates effective leaders and ensures sustainable success in coaching and development.

Chapter 10:

Next-Level Leadership Conversations

Your role as a mirror in coaching is far from passive. Unlike a static mirror, you're engaged in dynamic interaction, helping the coachee dissect and understand what they present. This requires keen observation and the ability to provide feedback that goes beyond surface-level reactions.

An effective mirror doesn't distort; it provides clarity. Similarly, your feedback should be clear and honest, but not harsh. It's about offering insights that are both understandable and supportive, providing a true (and compassionate) reflection of their actions and words.

A mirror reflects in real time—so should you. Focus on the present moment during coaching sessions, emphasising the immediate impact of the coachee's actions and words. This real-time feedback is essential for fostering self-awareness and enabling quick adjustment.

Engaging with the Mirror: A Two-Way Process

Just as one looks into a mirror to examine their appearance, encourage your coachee's to gaze into the 'mirror' you provide for scrutinising their thoughts and behaviours. Motivate them to pose questions to themselves, delve into their feelings, and critically analyse the reflections they observe.

Utilise reflective listening to demonstrate to your coachee's that you genuinely comprehend their perspective. This entails paraphrasing their words, posing clarifying questions, and expressing sincere empathy. It's akin to fine-tuning a mirror to ensure it reflects the most precise image. Just as a mirror can reveal different angles and depths, guide your coachee's to explore various facets of their issues.

Motivate them to change and broaden their viewpoint, perceive beyond the evident, and grasp the layered complexities of their behaviours and emotions.

Becoming a Reflective Surface

As a coach, your ability to provide reflective feedback is central to effective Mirror Coaching. Here's how you can refine this skill:

When a coachee shares their thoughts or feelings, your response should do more than echo. Think of yourself as a mirror that not only reflects but magnifies certain aspects to bring attention to them. Rephrasing their words in your own language isn't just about showing you're listening—it's about highlighting areas they might have overlooked. For example, if a coachee says, "I'm just not good in meetings," you might reflect, "You feel uncertain about your contributions in meetings?" This subtle shift prompts deeper self-reflection.

The principles of active listening and empathetic feedback draw inspiration from Carl Rogers' person-centred therapy [15]. This aspect underscores the importance of genuine engagement and constructive feedback, creating an environment where coachee's feel heard, understood, and motivated to explore deeper facets of their psyche.

The power of an open-ended question lies in its ability to pivot the mirror in different directions, illuminating unseen angles. Instead of leading to yes or no answers, these questions encourage coachee's to explore their thoughts and feelings more broadly. For instance, asking, "What aspects of your performance in meetings do you wish to improve?" opens a space for detailed introspection. It's like adjusting a mirror to reveal a part of themselves they haven't noticed before.

Just as a mirror accurately reflects what's in front of it, your listening should capture the essence of what the coachee is expressing. This involves not only hearing their words but also understanding the emotions and intentions behind them. Active listening requires you to be fully present, maintain eye contact, nod, and show that you are engaged. This reflective listening reassures the coachee that their feelings and thoughts are being seen and valued, just as one would appreciate a clear and accurate reflection in a mirror.

Mirroring isn't limited to words. Non-verbal cues—body language, tone, and facial expressions—also play a crucial role in effective reflection. Ensuring alignment between verbal and non-verbal communication strengthens trust and authenticity. Pay attention to these subtle cues, as they validate the coachee's feelings. For example, if a coachee appears anxious, your calm, attentive demeanor can reflect understanding and stability.

Deepening the Reflection

In Mirror Coaching, deepening the reflection is about enhancing the coachees self-awareness through a more profound engagement. Here's how to accomplish this:

Consider your role as a mirror that not only reflects but also interprets emotions and underlying meanings. When you mirror a coachees thoughts, infuse them with empathy. This involves understanding and appreciating the feelings behind their words and responding in a way that conveys this understanding.

For example, if a coachee expresses frustration about their performance, you might reflect, "It sounds like you're really being hard on yourself about this. What part of your performance felt most challenging?" This approach not only demonstrates that you're listening but also that you're connecting with their emotional state.

Your guidance should resemble a mirror that subtly adjusts to reveal blind spots. It's not about dictating to coachees what to do; it's about guiding them to see what they haven't yet observed in themselves. When nudging them towards realisations, frame your guidance as insights rather than instructions.

For instance, if a coachee is stuck in a specific mindset, you might say, "Have you considered examining this from a different perspective? What might you discover then?" This helps them explore new viewpoints without feeling directed or corrected.

Just as a mirror can unveil what's hiding in the background, use your questions and reflections to bring unnoticed aspects of the coachees behaviour or thought patterns to light. This could involve highlighting inconsistencies in their statements or drawing attention to recurring themes in their dialogue.

For example, if a coachee repeatedly criticises themselves, point out this pattern and ask, "What impact do you think this self-criticism has on your confidence?"

Encourage coachees to engage in reflective self-questioning, facilitating a deeper internal dialogue. This is akin to holding up a mirror for them to scrutinise their own thoughts and emotions more closely. Suggest reflective questions they can ponder, such as, "What does this reaction tell me about my core values or beliefs?"

By deepening the reflection in these ways, you empower coachees to gain a more nuanced and comprehensive understanding of themselves. This deeper engagement fosters greater self-awareness and insight, which are crucial for personal growth and development.

Clarifying and Sharpening Insights

In this phase of Mirror Coaching, the focus is on helping coachees clarify their thoughts and perceptions, much like a mirror that brings a blurred image into focus.

Think of your coaching role as a mirror that helps adjust the focus. When coachees have misconceptions or misinterpretations about their behaviour or situations, guide them gently towards clarity.

For example, if a coachee misinterprets a colleague's feedback as purely negative, you might prompt them to re-examine this perception: "Could there be a constructive element in that feedback you might have overlooked?" This approach encourages them to reconsider their initial interpretations and see the broader picture.

Your role is to help coachees see their true reflections—not what they imagine or fear. When they express self-doubt or biased views of their abilities, guide them to differentiate between perception and reality.

Ask questions like, "What evidence do you have to support this belief about yourself?" This not only challenges their assumptions but also guides them towards a more realistic and balanced self-view.

Use your reflective skills to highlight patterns in the coachees behaviour or thinking that they might not be aware of. For instance, if a coachee consistently attributes their successes to external factors, point out this tendency and explore its implications: "I've noticed you often credit your team for successes. How do you view your own contribution to these achievements?" This helps them recognise and reconsider recurring themes in their self-perception.

Like a mirror that shows an accurate image, encourage coachees to take ownership of their actions and their consequences. If a coachee is avoiding responsibility for a mistake, guide them towards acknowledgment and learning. Pose reflective questions like, "What could be your part in this situation, and what can you learn from it?" This promotes a sense of responsibility and growth. By focusing on these aspects, you assist coachees in turning their initial, perhaps vague or skewed, self-reflections into clearer, actionable insights. This clarity is crucial for their self-awareness and subsequent growth, just as a clear reflection in a mirror is essential for accurate perception.

Honest Feedback: The Unbiased Mirror

In the realm of Mirror Coaching, honest feedback is your tool for presenting a clear and unaltered reflection of the coachee's behaviours and thoughts. The feedback approach is derived from the Feedback Intervention Theory by Kluger and DeNisi [16] to underline the importance of providing feedback that is specific, task-oriented, and balanced. This ensures that feedback is a catalyst for growth and development, not just a commentary on performance.

Think of yourself as a mirror that should reflect without distortion. Your feedback will be honest and direct yet free from judgement. This involves commenting on behaviours and outcomes without attaching labels or criticisms.

For example, if a coachee consistently misses deadlines, instead of labelling them as 'irresponsible,' point out the pattern: "I've noticed that deadlines have been a challenge. Let's explore what's behind this pattern." This approach allows coachee's to see the consequences of their actions without feeling judged, encouraging introspection and change.

Like a mirror that shows exactly what's in front of it, your observations should be factual and based on specific instances or behaviours. Avoid generalisations and focus on concrete examples.

When discussing a coachee's tendency to dominate conversations, refer to specific instances: "In our last two sessions, I observed that you spoke for the majority of the time. How do you think this impacts the conversation flow?" This specificity helps coachee's recognise and understand the impact of their actions.

Use your feedback to encourage deeper self-reflection. Present your observations in a way that prompts coachee's to examine their behaviours and attitudes critically. For instance, if a coachee reacts defensively to feedback, you might say, "I noticed you seemed quite defensive when discussing this topic. What do you think triggered that reaction?" This kind of feedback acts like a mirror, offering coachee's a chance to see and understand their reactions and patterns.

Remember, a mirror reflects both flattering and unflattering images. Similarly, balance your feedback to include positive observations along with areas for improvement. This balanced approach ensures that coachee's don't feel overwhelmed by negative reflections and recognise their strengths and achievements.

For example, "While you've had challenges with meeting deadlines, your creativity in problem-solving has consistently added value to the project."

By adopting these approaches in providing feedback, you mirror reality in a way that is clear, honest, and conducive to growth. This helps individuals not only to accept their true selves but also to take constructive steps toward personal and professional development.

Perspective Shift: Adjusting the Mirror

In Mirror Coaching, facilitating a perspective shift in coachees is akin to adjusting a mirror to reveal different views. This shift can uncover new insights and understanding.

The task is to help coachee's tilt their mirror to see themselves and their situations from new angles. This might involve challenging them to consider the impact of their actions on others or to envision alternative outcomes to their usual approaches. For instance, if a Coachee is struggling with team dynamics, encourage them to reflect from a teammate's perspective: "If you were in your colleague's position, how would you view this situation?" This perspective shift can lead to empathy and a broader understanding of interpersonal dynamics.

Socratic questioning, inspired by a critical thinking framework, guides individuals toward greater self-reflection and broader exploration of their thoughts and behaviours.

This technique is exemplified in the crafting of five key questions, which help deepen understanding and encourage thoughtful introspection.[17]

Use your questions to guide coachees in exploring their issues from various vantage points. This broadened view can reveal unseen aspects of a problem or challenge. For example, ask, "What are some other ways you could interpret this feedback?" Such questions help coachees to step back from their immediate reactions and consider different interpretations, fostering a more comprehensive understanding of the situation.

Just as adjusting a mirror reveals new parts of a room, guiding coachees to adjust their perspective can uncover new possibilities. Encourage them to consider alternative strategies or viewpoints. For instance, if a coachee is fixated on a single solution, challenge them to brainstorm other options: "Let's explore other approaches. What other ways could you tackle this?"

Prompt coachees to reflect on how their actions and decisions impact others. This reflection is crucial in understanding the ripple effects of their behaviour. For instance, in a conflict situation, ask, "How do you think your approach affected the other person?" This encourages coachees to acknowledge the consequences of their actions and to consider more mindful and effective ways of interacting.

By guiding individuals to shift their perspectives, you are effectively helping them to adjust their mirrors, enabling them to see themselves and their situations from different angles. This adjustment reveals blind spots and broadens their understanding, opening new avenues for personal growth and development. Just as rear-view and wing mirrors provide a more comprehensive view of the road, this broader perspective helps individuals navigate their personal and professional journeys more effectively.

In Mirror Coaching, facilitating growth and change is about helping coaches see their evolving reflections over time, akin to how our image in a mirror changes as we grow. This perspective reveals how Mirror Coaching can significantly influence leadership development, performance improvement, and personal growth, aligning closely with the goals of frontline coaching.

Just as a person changes over the years, the reflections seen in coaching evolve. Emphasise to the coachee's that their self-perception at the beginning of coaching will likely shift as they progress. Encourage them to document these changes, perhaps through journaling or reflective exercises. For example, ask them to reflect on how their responses to certain situations have evolved: "Compare how you would have handled this situation a few months ago to your approach now. What differences do you notice?"

Your role is to guide coachee's through this transformation by acting like a mirror that adapts to their growth. Acknowledge and validate their progress, pointing out developments in their behaviour, thinking, or emotional responses.

This could involve recognising improvements in their communication skills, decision-making, or self-awareness: "I've observed a significant shift in how you communicate your ideas compared to when we started. What changes have you made to achieve this?"

Reinforce the concept that personal growth is an ongoing, dynamic process. Just as our reflection in a mirror changes with time and circumstances, so too does a person's self-awareness and behaviour. Encourage coachee to view their development as a continuous journey rather than a fixed destination. Use questions that prompt ongoing reflection: "As you continue to grow, what are some areas you want to focus on next?"

Like marking height changes on a wall next to a mirror, celebrate the milestones in your coachee's growth journey. Recognising and celebrating progress, whether it's handling a difficult conversation or improving stress management, reinforces their achievements and motivates further development.

These guided self-reflections are not linear but intertwined, creating a dynamic process that fosters self-awareness and growth. Throughout this journey, individuals and teams become architects of their own development, using the mirror of reflection, feedback, and perspective to guide them towards their fullest potential.

In the following sections, we will delve deeper into each stage, providing practical guidance on how to navigate this transformative process effectively. This not only enhances individual capabilities but also aligns behaviours with organisational goals and standards, fostering an environment of continuous improvement and development.

The intent behind these questions is to guide the coachee through a process of self-discovery and learning, enabling them to assess their performance and critically identify areas for growth. This approach helps develop their capabilities and align their behaviour with expected standards and goals. Through these questions, the coach facilitates a supportive environment where the coachee can openly reflect and plan for future development.

Case Study: "The Air Changed When She Walked In"

A Four-Session Mirror Coaching Journey

In this case study, we follow a frontline team leader—Naledi—over four coaching conversations guided by the five core Mirror Coaching Questions. Her story is not one of quick fixes or forced commitments. Instead, it illustrates something far more authentic: the slow, reflective shift from disconnection to presence; from control to influence.

The journey reveals how powerful it is to hold the mirror steady, resist the urge to rescue, and trust the leader to find their way forward.

Session 1: Seeing the Consequences

Naledi had become sharp and withdrawn with her team. While her targets were still met, her team had gone quiet. When Norma, her supervisor, sat her down, she didn't come with correction—she came with a mirror.

"People are avoiding you. They say the room changes when you speak. That used to not be the case."

Naledi resisted at first— "I'm just pushing for results." But when Norma asked her to name the consequences of that tone, she slowly admitted:

"They stop talking to me. They do the minimum. I'm losing their trust."

There was no solution offered. No plan drawn up. Just a pause. A crack in the old identity. And a whisper of awareness:
"I don't want to be that kind of leader."

Session 2: Choosing to Return

Four days later, Naledi returned—thoughtful, watchful. She'd begun noticing her own behaviour in real time. She said, "I didn't fix everything, but I saw the moments. I saw the hesitation in them—and in me."

She had started one small experiment: pausing before she responded. Giving her team space to speak. Norma reflected it back:
"You created space. That's leadership."

They revisited the earlier tension, and the cost of control.

"If I grip too tightly, they stop thinking. I lead alone. I burn out."

No one told her that. She saw it. And she believed it. That's when change became possible.

Session 3: Stumbling Without Starting Over

A week later, Naledi came back discouraged. Under pressure, she'd snapped again. Her tone had slipped. But something was different.

"This time, I caught it. I apologised. I've never done that before."

Rather than judge the slip, Norma helped her reflect:

"What did that moment cost you? And what did your recovery earn you?"

Naledi paused.
"It didn't fix everything. But it told them I care. That I'm trying."

She named a new practice: not just pausing—but resetting out loud. Letting the team see her try again. She wasn't hiding anymore.

Session 4: A Felt Shift

Two weeks later, things felt different—not perfect, but grounded. The team was speaking more. Someone even challenged her idea in a meeting—and she welcomed it.

"I used to think leadership was about having the answers. Now I think it's about holding the room."

Norma asked what she was proud of.

"I didn't force anything. I gave space—and they filled it."

Naledi's growth wasn't flashy. She hadn't solved everything. But she had changed the air around her—and that was the beginning of sustainable leadership.

Open Questions That Change the Way People Grow

Most coaching models break down because they skip the thinking. The leader talks, the coachee nods, and no real learning happens. Mirror Coaching corrects that. It's not about quick fixes—it's about building internal processing habits that drive performance, ownership, and belief over time. The five questions in this model aren't just helpful—they are sequenced to activate reflection, reinforce confidence, surface accountability, embed belief, and move forward with clarity.

Let's walk through the sequence—not just the questions, but the why behind the order.

Step 1: Self-Reflection

"How do you think you went with that?"
This is the mirror being raised. It's where learning begins. If you skip this step and go straight to feedback, you've taken away their chance to think—and your coaching becomes a monologue, not a learning loop. This question invites self-perception. If they overestimate their performance, you know belief needs recalibration. If they underestimate, confidence needs restoring.

Prescriptive Coaching Cue:
Never open with your verdict. Let them speak first—and let the silence do the work.

Step 2: Celebrate Success

"What do you think you did well?"
Growth doesn't start from deficiency. It starts from strength. This second question grounds the reflection in confidence. It reminds the coachee they already have what it takes—they just need to apply it more consistently. This is especially critical in high-pressure roles, where feedback can often feel like a trap. When you start here, you create psychological safety and reframe feedback as opportunity, not punishment.

Prescriptive Coaching Cue:
Name something positive—even in a tough moment. It changes the tone of the entire conversation.

Step 3: Identify Gaps

"What do you think you didn't do well?"
Only now—after space for reflection and a strength anchor—can you shift the lens to challenge. At this point, the coachee is more open, more honest, and more likely to self-diagnose accurately. Done in the wrong order, this question feels like blame. Done now, it feels like growth.

Let them lead here. If they miss something, you still have space to guide later. But the goal is ownership—not dependence on your judgement.

Prescriptive Coaching Cue:
Let them speak without sugar-coating or prompting. You're listening for ownership—not perfection.

Step 4: Explore Consequences

"What do you think the consequences of that were?"
This is the pivotal question. Without it, most coaching loops become transactional—focused on tasks, not transformation. When you ask this question, you invite the coachee to connect their behaviour to its ripple effect: on safety, on team dynamics, on delivery. This is where belief is built—not just in the task, but in the why behind it.

Prescriptive Coaching Cue:
Never skip this. Don't give advice yet. Let the weight of their own answer do the work. You're helping them see impact—not just fix behaviour.

Step 5: Commit to Action

"What's one thing you'll do differently next time?"
The final step moves from insight to commitment. After reflecting, acknowledging, and feeling the weight of impact, most coachees are ready to act. The question becomes natural—almost obvious. But without the groundwork, this

step falls flat. You'll get vague answers, or they'll wait for you to solve it. That's not growth—it's dependency.

Prescriptive Coaching Cue:
Let them own the next step. Only guide if they miss the mark. You're shaping confidence, not control.

Why This Order Matters

Each question in this sequence is deliberate. Skip one, and you compromise the internal process:

- Skip the first, and there's no reflection.

- Skip the second, and there's no confidence.

- Skip the third, and there's no ownership.

- Skip the fourth, and there's no belief.

- Skip the fifth, and there's no change.

This method builds habits of thinking. Over time, the questions become part of how the team talks, reviews, and leads—without you needing to facilitate every moment. When people start saying these questions out loud—unprompted, at handovers, in peer feedback—you'll know the loop has taken root.

This is what coaching maturity looks like:

- When your team reflects before you ask.

- When they act before they're told.

- When they internalise the standard—not because they were managed, but because they believe in it.

Reflective Practice Prompt

Use the Mirror Coaching Sequence in your next coaching moment. Afterward, reflect:

- Which question felt hardest to hold?

- Did the coachee offer insight before you intervened?

- Did their commitment feel real—or rehearsed?

Remember: growth lives in the tension. Don't collapse it too early. Hold it with care—and let clarity rise

Chapter 11:

When Feedback Becomes a System

What Feedback Is—And What It Is Not

Feedback is one of the most misunderstood tools in frontline leadership. For many, it still carries the flavour of correction—something a manager gives when something goes wrong, or when someone needs to be set straight. That misunderstanding turns feedback into a weapon of authority rather than a lever for development. And as a result, people learn to avoid it, brace against it, or comply with it just enough to get through the moment. But none of those responses build competence. None of them deepen awareness. And none of them turn feedback into a habit that scales.

To build a strong coaching system, leaders must begin with a clear definition: feedback is structured reflection that helps someone see what they didn't see before—and equips them to respond differently next time. It's not commentary. It's not advice-giving. It's not about reviewing the person's performance or explaining what should have happened. Good feedback is not a lecture. It is not a speech. It is not a checklist of faults or an emotional download.

What feedback *is*—when done well—is a mirror. It helps the person look again, from a different angle. It offers the chance to connect action to impact. And most importantly, it creates space for ownership. That's why good feedback is not something you do *to* someone—it's something you invite them into. It's a moment of co-learning. The insight might begin with the coach, but the learning belongs to the coachee.

This means the purpose of feedback is not to make a point. It is to help the person grow. Feedback exists to sharpen judgment, expand awareness, and build confidence in how someone chooses to act. Its role is to increase competence—not just in that moment, but over time. When feedback works, it creates the conditions for capability to emerge.

One of the most powerful things feedback does is uncover what the person may not have realised. That might be a gap in attention, a missed detail, a broken habit, or a subconscious behaviour that's now visible. Psychologists refer to this shift in terms of a lens that describes how people move from unconscious to conscious awareness. What was hidden from view becomes visible. What was automatic becomes deliberate. Feedback is the mechanism that opens that window—if delivered well.

But when feedback is used poorly, the opposite happens. The window closes. The person shuts down. They retreat into self-protection or performance mimicry. They may agree, but they're not learning. That's why feedback must be structured, safe, and meaningful. If the goal is capability, then the process must support thinking—not just compliance.

It's also important to remember that not everything that sounds like feedback actually is. Vague praise isn't feedback. Saying "good job" without context teaches nothing. General criticism isn't feedback either. Saying "you need to be more careful" might feel like guidance, but it leaves the person without a clear sense of what to adjust. True feedback is grounded in specifics. It references what was seen or heard. It connects the dots between action and effect. It asks for reflection. And it supports a practical, visible change.

When feedback is framed this way—as a structured learning conversation—it starts to feel different. It becomes something people don't just tolerate, but value. They begin to see it as part of how they get better—not a test of how they're doing. And that shift changes everything. It's the difference between fear and curiosity. Between avoidance and initiative. Between repeat mistakes and repeatable learning.

As a coach, your job is not to wait for something to go wrong before offering feedback. Nor is it to deliver it as a final verdict. Your job is to make feedback a normal part of how people learn, think, and grow in their role. That starts with how you define it. Because what you believe feedback is will shape how you deliver it—and how it is received.

The Purpose Is Growth

Feedback is not just a performance tool—it is a growth tool. That distinction matters. Because if you see feedback as something to correct behaviour or ensure compliance, then your delivery will become transactional. But if you see feedback as something that builds capacity and unlocks potential, your entire approach will change. Feedback then becomes a form of investment, not inspection.

At its core, the purpose of feedback is to help someone grow. Not just to meet today's task requirement, but to strengthen tomorrow's judgment, ownership, and skill. Done well, feedback increases competence over time. It supports the small adjustments that make big differences later. It helps the person move from dependent execution to independent thinking. It develops internal self-correction rather than external supervision.

This is why coaching and feedback must go hand in hand. Coaching builds belief. Feedback builds clarity. Coaching supports motivation. Feedback supports decision-making. The two must work together if the goal is sustainable, repeatable, and self-driven performance.

Yet in many workplaces, feedback is still treated as something you give after a mistake—or as part of a review process. It becomes something reactive, corrective, and occasional. That approach keeps the person in reactive mode too. They wait for the leader to spot the issue. They wait to be told. And in doing so, they miss the opportunity to build awareness for themselves. That's the real cost of underused or misused feedback—not just the mistake itself, but the lost opportunity to develop.

The strength of feedback is not in how clever the coach sounds. It lies in how clearly the person begins to think differently. It opens the moment where someone goes, *"Ah— I didn't realise that was the impact of what I did."* That spark of awareness is the beginning of behavioural shift. And once that reflection starts, capability can grow.

When this reflection becomes habitual, something else happens: people begin to expect feedback. They start to invite it. They stop bracing for it as if it were a correction and start using it as a lever. That's when feedback moves from being a leadership function to a team habit.

Research supports this shift. *"Feedback becomes safer, more effective, and more intrinsically motivating when it shifts from judgment to structured insight"* [18]. When people experience feedback as a tool to help them grow— rather than a judgment of how they've failed—they engage differently. They listen with openness. They reflect more deeply. And they act with greater clarity and intent.

That's the true purpose of feedback. It's not to get someone to follow the rule. It's to help them understand why the rule matters—and how to act on it with conviction. It doesn't just tell someone what to do. It helps them decide how to do it well. That's what grows capability. That's what builds culture. And that's what makes feedback not just an act of communication—but a system of learning.

It Is Not a Reset

In many teams, feedback still functions like a circuit breaker. Something goes wrong, a leader intervenes, and a correction is issued. For a moment, the problem appears to be fixed. The team adjusts, the shift resumes, and the issue seems resolved—until it happens again. The same lapse returns a few days later, often under similar conditions. And the cycle repeats itself: spot, fix, repeat.

This is what happens when feedback is treated as a reset button. It corrects the moment, but it doesn't strengthen the system. There's no reflection, no shift in thinking, and no change in internal awareness. The leader may feel like they've acted, but the person has not learned. As a result, performance becomes leader-dependent. Standards only hold when someone is watching. And that is not capability—it's conditional compliance.

To break that pattern, feedback must be repositioned. It must stop being a one-off event and start becoming a consistent, visible rhythm. When feedback becomes a system, it no longer relies on the presence of the leader to drive improvement. It lives in the way the team thinks, reflects, and chooses—on their own. That's the difference between enforcement and belief.

Feedback as a system means that it is not occasional. It is not reserved for performance reviews, audit outcomes, or moments of failure. It happens daily. It happens during task reviews, walk-throughs, toolbox talks, shift handovers, and job debriefs. It becomes embedded in the routine. And because it is frequent, it becomes normal. When that happens, feedback no longer signals something went wrong—it signals that learning is ongoing.

It also means that feedback follows a structure. Not a script, but a recognisable pattern. That structure could be the OILS model, a set of coaching questions, or a shared team habit. The point is predictability. When people know how feedback will be delivered, they stop fearing it. They stop bracing. And that shift alone changes the dynamic of the conversation. It moves the person from protection to participation.

The key mindset here is that feedback should not reset performance—it should progress it. It should take the person forward, not send them back to the starting line. This requires more than a correction. It requires connection: between the action, the impact, and the belief underneath it. When that connection is made visible, the person learns. And when it is made consistently, the system learns.

Leaders who understand this begin to operate differently. They no longer wait for mistakes to intervene. They no longer coach only when something breaks. They begin to coach as a design practice—as a way to embed standards into how people think and act, not just into what they do. And over time, that changes everything. Because when feedback is built into the rhythm, it starts to shape the culture. And when feedback becomes culture, leadership becomes scalable.

It's one thing to give feedback. It's another to make sure it lands.

Many leaders believe that saying the right thing is enough—that once the message is delivered, the job is done. But that's not how learning works. What matters in feedback is not just what is said, but how it is received. And the way feedback is delivered shapes everything about whether it sticks, whether it's resisted, or whether it gets buried under shame, confusion, or silence.

The first principle of effective delivery is neutrality. Feedback is not a performance. It's not an emotional verdict. It is a leadership act that must be delivered with calm, respect, and focus. That doesn't mean avoiding honesty. It means delivering truth without threat. The leader's tone should be adult-to-adult—never condescending, sarcastic, or rushed. *"You didn't follow the standard again"* sounds accusatory. *"I noticed we skipped the pre-task check"* is factual. The difference is discipline in delivery.

The second principle is specificity. Vague statements teach nothing. They trigger confusion, and worse, they leave the person to fill in the blanks—usually with the harshest version of what they think you meant. Feedback should name the exact behaviour observed, not a guess about intent or character. It should align to something known: a checklist, a protocol, a role expectation. When the person can connect your feedback to something concrete, their mind shifts from defence to understanding.

The third principle is timing. Some feedback moments need to happen in the moment. Others need a pause. Leaders must learn to read both. Immediate feedback works when the environment is calm, the issue is fresh, and there is space for conversation. But when emotions are elevated or the moment is public, delay may serve better than haste. A quiet conversation five minutes later—delivered privately—can carry ten times the impact of a public correction. Feedback is not urgent by default. It is important. And importance demands intentional timing.

Environment also matters. Where you choose to speak tells the person how seriously to take the message—and how much dignity they will be offered in the process. Public correction often creates embarrassment. Private coaching fosters reflection. Even saying, *"Let's take two minutes on this outside,"* signals care. The setting you choose either protects the person's self-respect or puts it at risk. And when dignity is at risk, learning shuts down.

Finally, feedback should not be a one-sided monologue. The best feedback is interactive. It invites the person into reflection. It gives them a chance to speak, not just listen. A coach does not fill every space with instruction—they use space. They allow the person to process, to think, and to connect the dots for themselves. That's where ownership begins.

Leaders who want feedback to land must slow down. They must stop trying to win the conversation or prove their point. They must stop coaching from frustration. Feedback that sticks is feedback that supports learning. And learning only happens when the conditions are right: clear language, calm tone, visible standard, safe setting, and space to reflect.

That is how feedback becomes effective. That is how it lands—not as pressure, but as purpose.

A Repeatable Framework

Feedback must be more than a reaction. It needs rhythm. It needs structure. Not to script the coach—but to support the learner. Without structure, feedback becomes inconsistent: sometimes vague, sometimes emotional, sometimes skipped altogether. But with a clear framework, feedback becomes repeatable, teachable, and reliable. It becomes something teams come to expect—not fear. That's where the OILS model comes in.

OILS stands for Observation, Impact, Listening, and Suggestions. Each step plays a different role. Together, they create a complete learning conversation—one that invites reflection, prompts ownership, and reinforces standards without triggering shame.

Observation: What Was Seen or Heard

Feedback begins with naming the observable behaviour or event. This step must be neutral and specific. The goal here is not to guess motivation or interpret emotion. It's simply to surface what happened, so both parties can begin from a shared understanding.

> *"I noticed we moved into the prestart meeting without covering today's safety focus."*
>
> Alternate phrasing: *"I saw the checklist was opened, but we didn't talk through the key risks before starting."*

This step matters because it anchors the conversation in fact, not judgment. It reduces defensiveness. It removes guesswork. And it gives the coachee something concrete to reflect on.

Impact: What Resulted Because of It

Once the behaviour is named, the coach helps the person see what followed. This step is critical. Many lapses on the frontline are not deliberate—they're habitual. The person may not realise what their action triggered. Impact opens that blind spot. It creates the link between what happened and what that action caused.

> *"Because that safety point wasn't discussed, we started the task without flagging the confined space risk. That left the team unprepared."*

> Alternate phrasing: *"Skipping that item meant one of our main hazards went undiscussed—we missed a chance to set the right tone."*

This is the moment where feedback becomes meaningful. It shifts the conversation from correction to consequence. It shows that the missed step wasn't minor—it mattered. And when someone realises that, they begin to see their role differently.

It is known that people operate within blind spots—unseen aspects of their behaviour or its impact. Feedback at the Impact stage helps reduce those blind spots. It creates conscious awareness where there was none. That's when the mindset begins to pivot.

Listening: What They Think About It

After naming what was observed and the consequence it created, the leader must pause. This is the moment where reflection begins. The coach's role here is to invite the person into the conversation—not to control it.

> *"What was happening for you in that moment?"*
>
> *"Do you think that step got missed, or was it skipped on purpose?"*
>
> *"Looking back, what do you think was going through the team's mind?"*

These questions are not designed to test or trap. They're designed to create space. When someone starts to reflect, their words reveal what they believe, what they missed, or what they assumed. And when that thinking becomes visible, the coach can work with it.

This step is often skipped—but it's the most important part of the learning cycle. It's where ownership begins.

Suggestions: What They'll Do Differently

The final step is forward-facing. It's not about wrapping up with a lecture or a fix. It's about giving the person a chance to name the improvement themselves. This is where commitment forms.

> *"What could help you remember that safety focus next time?"*
>
> *"Would it work to have that prompt listed on your whiteboard?"*
>
> *"Let's add that into the checklist together—do you agree with that step?"*

When people name the improvement themselves, it sticks. It becomes their idea. Their action. Their standard. And when they struggle to name it clearly, the coach can support—but not override. The goal is a clear, shared next step that reinforces belief and sets the standard visibly for next time.

Used consistently, OILS becomes more than a model—it becomes a language. Teams begin to anticipate the rhythm: *"What did we see? What did it cause? What do we think? What will we do?"* And that rhythm begins to rewire the system. Feedback stops being emotional. It becomes part of how we think. And that's when belief turns into behaviour that lasts.

How to Receive

Feedback is not just a skill to give—it is also a posture to receive. And that's often the harder part. Because when feedback is personal, unexpected, or delivered clumsily, the natural response isn't insight. It's emotion.

Even the most confident team members can feel exposed when they're being observed. When someone points out a missed step or asks for a better standard, it triggers more than a thought—it triggers a feeling. That feeling might be embarrassment, frustration, defensiveness, or shame. Sometimes the reaction is visible. Sometimes it's buried. But it's there. And that's what makes receiving feedback a leadership act in itself.

The first thing to understand is that the emotional response is not failure. It is human. The brain is wired to protect identity and preserve pride. When feedback arrives—especially in moments of fatigue, surprise, or self-doubt—the protective mind activates first. The person may deflect, downplay, overexplain, or go quiet. Not because they're resisting change, but because they're still processing what was said and what it means.

This is where self-awareness matters most. A coach who receives feedback well is someone who understands that reflection often comes after reaction. They allow themselves a moment. They breathe. They don't rush to respond or fix. They let the emotional energy settle before trying to process the lesson inside it.

That moment of pause is what separates growth from guilt. It's what keeps the feedback from becoming a threat and turns it into an opportunity. It might sound like: *"Thanks for that—I need a second to think through what you just said."* Or: *"That's hard to hear, but I'm hearing you. Let me reflect before I respond."* These are not signs of weakness. They are signals of maturity. They show that the person is committed to learning, even when the learning stings.

This maturity is essential—especially for those in leadership roles. Teams don't just observe what you say. They observe how you receive correction, how you hold space when the spotlight is on you, and how you respond when your own standards slip. If you model defensiveness, they'll mimic it. If you model reflection, they'll absorb that too. That's how culture spreads—through visible patterns, not stated values.

There is also a deeper opportunity here. Leaders who receive feedback well create psychological safety in their teams. They signal that feedback is not a threat. It's a tool. And that signal invites others to participate in the process too. This is supported by research: *"Employees are more likely to engage with feedback when they see leaders modelling reflective behaviour and showing openness to growth, rather than control or defensiveness"* [19]. In other words, feedback is not just something you give—it's something you model.

To receive feedback like a coach, a few shifts are required. First, assume intent. Even if the delivery is imperfect, try to find the insight inside the message. Second, slow the moment down. Give yourself space to think before you speak. Third, reflect aloud. Share your thinking process so others can see what self-awareness looks like. And finally, act. Name the adjustment you'll make. Show that feedback doesn't just inform—it transforms.

In time, this posture becomes part of how you lead. You stop fearing feedback. You start using it. And as you model that shift, your team does too. That's when feedback stops being a performance conversation—and starts becoming a leadership culture.

Making It Work

Just as hand hygiene protects health, feedback hygiene protects culture. It is the quiet discipline that separates helpful feedback from harmful commentary. It's what keeps coaching moments clear, respectful, and productive—even when the topic is uncomfortable.

Feedback hygiene refers to the daily leadership habits that ensure feedback is delivered with clarity, care, and consistency. It's not a checklist for perfection—it's a foundation for trust. And without it, even the best intentions can land the wrong way.

The first hygiene habit is **clarity**. Feedback should be anchored in observable behaviour. Not assumptions. Not personality traits. And never emotion disguised as analysis. Saying, *"You always rush through tasks"* is vague and confrontational. Saying, *"I noticed that we skipped the equipment inspection step before the task"* is factual and constructive. The clearer the observation, the cleaner the conversation.

The second habit is **alignment to standards**. Feedback should connect to something real: a procedure, a checklist, a defined expectation. Without this anchor, feedback feels like opinion. And when feedback feels subjective, people are more likely to push back—or simply dismiss it. A well-grounded statement might sound like: *"The job card requires us to verify the isolations. That step wasn't confirmed before work began."* This is not a personal judgment—it's a gap against a known standard.

The third hygiene habit is **neutral tone**. Leadership tone matters more than leaders often realise. Frustration, sarcasm, or emotional tone distort the message and raise the emotional temperature. When tone becomes reactive, the content becomes irrelevant—because the person is no longer listening. A neutral, steady delivery sends a signal: *"This is important, but it's safe to talk about."* That is the space in which learning happens.

Fourth is **the setting**. Feedback given in public—especially when corrective—can trigger embarrassment and resistance. That doesn't mean every conversation needs to be behind closed doors. But it does mean leaders must be intentional. Even a moment of privacy, like stepping aside or lowering your voice, can preserve the person's dignity. And when dignity is preserved, reflection is possible.

Fifth is **timing**. Leaders must learn the difference between urgency and effectiveness. Giving feedback too late weakens the connection to the event. Giving it too soon—when emotions are still high—can close the conversation before it begins. The best leaders pause long enough to choose the right moment, without using that pause as an excuse to avoid the conversation entirely. Feedback hygiene means being deliberate, not delayed.

The final hygiene habit is **frequency**. Feedback must be routine, not reserved. If it only shows up during audits or annual reviews, it becomes a threat signal. But if it happens daily—during walkabouts, handovers, shift briefings—it becomes a source of rhythm. It builds a culture where reflection is normal and learning is continuous.

These habits do not require extra time. They require intention. And when practiced regularly, they create something powerful: a workplace where people know what to expect, how to grow, and how to engage with leadership without fear.

Because in the end, feedback hygiene isn't about being nice. It's about being clear. It's not about softening the truth—it's about strengthening the process. When the structure of feedback is respected, the substance of feedback begins to stick. And that's when the culture starts to shift—not because of one conversation, but because of the way every conversation is held.

Chapter 12:

Leader Standard Work Is Core Work

Frontline leaders don't lack good intentions. Most want to coach. Most see its value. They often start the week with a mental note to "get out there more" or "check in with the crew." But by midweek, urgent tasks pile up, problems escalate, and coaching slips to the background. Not because it's unimportant. But because it wasn't scheduled.

Core truth is that if coaching doesn't live in your calendar, it won't live in your leadership.

Intentions are invisible; rhythms are not. Coaching becomes real when it has a place, a time, and a visible anchor in how you lead your week. Without this structure, coaching remains reactive—something done when there is a problem or if time permits. And time rarely permits. This is why rhythm matters more than strategy. Even the most effective coaching method will not take hold if it appears only sporadically—if feedback is given only after failure or if observation happens only when meetings end early.

Consistency is more than a habit—it is a signal. Your team learns from what you prioritise. If they see coaching time protected, repeated, and honoured, they begin to treat it with the same seriousness. If they see you skip it for administrative work, they will learn to do the same with their standards. That's why this chapter doesn't just talk about coaching habits—it focuses on **the rhythm that sustains them.** Leadership is built in pattern. And that pattern must include space to observe, reflect, engage, coach, and course-correct—on purpose.

Think of coaching as part of your operating system. Not an add-on. Not a flavour-of-the-month. Not a thing you squeeze in.This structured approach is known as *Leader*

Standard Work—a disciplined way of working where leadership actions are planned in advance, executed with intent, and repeated consistently over time. It ensures that key leadership behaviours—such as coaching, observing, and reinforcing standards—are not left to chance, but are deliberately built into the rhythm of each week.

When coaching becomes a visible part of how you lead your week, it naturally becomes a visible part of how your team performs theirs. That is the shift this chapter will help you make—starting with the structure behind your leadership calendar. Most leaders do not fail to coach because they lack commitment; they fail to coach because their calendars do not make space for it. And over time, what is not visible in your schedule becomes invisible in your leadership.

In operational environments, standard work is how frontline teams deliver consistency: set sequences, clear expectations, repeatable tasks. Leader Standard Work applies that same logic to leadership behaviour. It takes coaching—often seen as a "soft skill"—and embeds it into **hard structure**.

If you treat coaching as an optional or reactive task, it will always get pushed aside when things get busy. But if you design coaching into your weekly rhythm—with time blocks, cues, and rituals—it becomes repeatable. More importantly, it becomes **observable to others**. Your calendar becomes a behavioural teaching tool. Think of it as the scaffolding that supports visible leadership. It's not about rigid schedules or micromanagement. It's about building **habitual visibility**—so that coaching doesn't rely on mood, memory, or capacity. It relies on rhythm

What Weekly Coaching Habits Should Include

Every frontline leader's schedule is different. But the building blocks of effective coaching rhythm are surprisingly universal. They include:

- **Field presence windows**
  → Time blocks where you are intentionally in the

field—not managing, but observing, asking, coaching. This could be 30 minutes each morning walking the floor with purpose, clipboard down, eyes up.

- **Crew alignment or shift-start coaching**
  → A quick 5–10 minute check-in with your team, not just to allocate tasks but to reinforce behaviours, standards, or safety priorities.

- **Weekly 1:1s or development chats**
  → Even 15-minute capability conversations each week keep growth visible. These should be focused, not fluffy—structured around improvement themes, not generic check-ins.

- **End-of-week coaching reflection**
  → A short session to ask: Who did I coach this week? What insights were surfaced? What needs reinforcement? This anchors your development focus and makes coaching trackable—not guesswork.

- **Calendar-based nudges or cues**
  → Use visual prompts—flags, colours, coaching notes. Anything that helps you remember: this is part of my leadership work—not admin, not extra.

When coaching becomes a leadership habit—anchored in weekly practice—it gains traction. Your team starts to recognise the rhythm. They prepare for it. They expect it. And over time, they **begin to internalise it**. Even better, it sends a clear cultural message: that development is not occasional, it's operational. That coaching is not what happens when something breaks—it's what builds people before they break.

This rhythm is not just for your team—it is for you. When coaching is done regularly, it sharpens your eye for detail, provides real-time insight into performance, and keeps you connected to the daily realities your crew faces. It also signals clearly that growth is not separate from the work—it is the work. You are not waiting for a performance issue to arise before coaching; you are coaching to prevent the issue from occurring in the first place. That is proactive leadership. That is coaching by design.

Coaching should be treated with the same discipline you would apply to any key operating procedure: it must be visible, repeated, measurable, and anchored in time—not just in good intention. When coaching becomes a standard part of your week, it becomes a standard part of your team's growth. Every leader has the same challenge: **not enough time for everything, but just enough time for what matters most.** The question is never whether you're busy. The question is whether your busyness reflects your leadership priorities—or just your firefighting reflex.

That's where the **Three Calendar Buckets** come in. This framework helps frontline leaders categorise their week by priority and purpose. It turns the abstract idea of "fitting in coaching" into a structured, manageable, and realistic system. Because let's be honest—if everything is urgent, coaching will never feel like it deserves a slot. But if coaching is your leadership, then it deserves to live in all three buckets.

Bucket 1: Must-Do Work (Role-Critical Activities)

These are the **non-negotiables**—the tasks, routines, or leadership moments that you are **accountable for delivering** every week, no matter what.

This includes:

- Field coaching walks scheduled and visible on the calendar

- Safety interactions or behavioural observations tied to leadership KPIs

- One-on-one development check-ins for direct reports

- Coaching conversations triggered by incidents, trends, or breakdowns

- Morning prep or shift-start meetings where you reinforce standards

You don't try to "make time" for these. You protect time for them. These coaching moments are part of the role. They're not "nice to do." They're **how you do the job well**.

Key practice: Block these into your calendar before anything else. Treat them like leadership production time—not discretionary effort.

Bucket 2: Flexible Work (Discretionary but Important)

This bucket includes the coaching work that is still valuable, but more responsive and timing-dependent. It includes:

- Ad hoc coaching moments in the field when you spot a teachable opportunity

- Supporting new team members through onboarding or task reviews

- Running small coaching huddles when systems stall or roles drift

- Facilitating improvement sessions or after-action reviews

You won't always know when these will happen—but you must make sure they happen regularly. These are the moments that **strengthen culture**. The difference is, you need to plan space to respond—not plan the exact content.

Key practice: Build flexible coaching windows into your weekly plan. Leave 30–60 minutes free daily to respond to what the field presents. Don't fill every hour with meetings. Protect the margin to lead.

Bucket 3: Growth Work (Developmental and Future-Focused)

This is where great leaders stretch others—and themselves. It's the least urgent but often the most powerful bucket for **long-term capability building**.

It includes:

- Strategic coaching around behaviours that need to evolve

- Time invested in upcoming team leads, potential successors, or future supervisors

- Reviewing coaching logs to track trends and patterns

- Reflecting on your coaching style and where it's landing—or not

- Holding forward-looking development sessions that don't solve today's task but shape tomorrow's capacity

This work is often what disappears when things get hectic. But it's also the work that multiplies you. It turns coaching from an activity into an investment. And without this bucket, the others just keep reacting.

A key practice is to book at least one hour per week specifically for growth work. Name it clearly. Protect it deliberately. And use it to build depth—not just to keep pace. This three-bucket model is not about achieving perfection; it is about developing awareness of your priorities. It helps you rebalance when the week becomes unpredictable. It gives you language to explain—to others and to yourself—why coaching time matters. And most importantly, it ensures that leadership remains structured, not merely hopeful. When coaching exists only in the reactive space, it reinforces a culture of correction. But when it is intentionally spread across all three buckets—deliberate, responsive, and developmental—it evolves into a sustainable leadership rhythm.

That is how performance truly shifts—not through a single heroic coaching moment, but through a consistent, well-balanced pattern of presence, thoughtful questioning, belief reinforcement, and deliberate development of the next level of thinking. Coaching does not demand more time; it demands better design. When coaching is structured intentionally into the rhythm of leadership, it becomes both scalable and sustainable.

This model helps you build exactly that. In any operational environment, if something is not protected, it gets consumed. Whether it is buffer time in a production schedule, safety barriers around a high-risk area, or designated crew rest periods—protection is a leadership act. Coaching is no different. If you want coaching to be consistent, it must be protected. The protected coaching window is a designated block of time within your leadership rhythm that is non-negotiable. It is not to be filled with administrative tasks, absorbed by meetings, or overridden by quick questions. It is time set aside—visible and intentional—for you to do what only leaders can do: coach, develop, and sharpen capability..

This is more than time management. It's **a cultural cue.** It signals to your team—and to you—that coaching is not an afterthought. It's a core activity, planned and prioritised. And when people see you protect that time, they begin to understand that development is not what you do when things go wrong. It's what you do to keep things going right.

What Does a Protected Coaching Window Look Like?

It's usually short. But it's sacred.

- **15–30 minutes each day** to observe a task, ask reflective questions, and give real-time feedback.

- **A recurring weekly field walk**, where your only goal is to listen, learn, and coach.

- **A blocked coaching hour** once a week where you rotate through team members to uplift skills—not just solve problems.

- **A slot just before or after shift start** where you embed one high-impact coaching conversation.

The length matters less than the intent. It's not about doing more—it's about being **present on purpose**.

How to Protect This Time

Let's be realistic: your week is full of competing demands. So how do you protect this window without becoming rigid or unrealistic?

Here's how high-performing leaders do it:

- **Name the block in your calendar.** Don't call it "Admin." Call it "Coaching Window" or "Capability Check-In." This makes it visible and intentional.

- **Communicate your plan.** Tell your team: "I'll be doing coaching rounds at 10am. I'm not checking up—I'm showing up." That removes suspicion and builds openness.

- **Honour the window like you would a meeting with your manager.** Would you skip a one-on-one with your leader for a last-minute task? No. So don't do it to your team.

- **Use it for reflection, not just correction.** Don't only show up when things go wrong. Use protected time to recognise good habits, ask what's working, and reinforce standards.

- **Log your insights.** A quick voice note or one-line coaching note after each session helps you track growth patterns over time. This isn't bureaucracy—it's memory.

Coaching doesn't scale unless it's routine. And routines don't hold unless they're protected.

This window becomes the anchor for coaching visibility. When your team knows they'll see you in the field, asking questions and offering feedback, they start preparing. They raise their standards. They start self-assessing before you arrive. And over time, they become less dependent on your presence—because your **coaching rhythm has become their performance rhythm**.

IIt is not just about doing more coaching—it is about making coaching matter more, because it is consistent, visible, and respected. In operational leadership, a protected coaching window is one of the highest-leverage time investments you can make. It builds culture, strengthens habits, and communicates—without needing to say a word—that development is part of the job. The case has already been made: coaching is not something you "try to fit in." It is something you lead through. It should be visible, scheduled, and structured into your calendar like any other high-impact operational activity. But what does that actually look like across a real week?

Let's walk through an example of what a **well-structured coaching week** might include for a frontline leader. This isn't about filling every hour. It's about making coaching habitual, not heroic. Consistent, not chaotic.

Monday

- **07:30 – Field Check-in & Intentional Observation (30 min)**
  Start the week with presence. You're not there to inspect—you're there to understand. Ask one coaching question:

  "What's the one thing we need to get right this week?"

- **13:00 – Protected Coaching Window (30 min)**
  Choose one task, one team, or one person. Give feedback using the OILS model. Document the insight briefly.

- **End-of-day – Calendar Review (15 min)**
  Ask yourself: "Where this week is my leadership showing up through coaching?" Adjust as needed.

Tuesday

- **Shift Start – Safety Interaction with Reflection (25 min)**
  Don't just ask if the PPE is correct. Ask:

  "What are the consequences of missing one step today?"
  Build belief, not just checklist compliance.

- **Midday – Spot Coaching in the Field (20 min)**
  Observe a small task. Use Mirror Coaching Questions. Let the coachee lead the close.

Wednesday

- **07:45 – Team Huddle with a Coaching Focus (25 min)**
  Anchor the conversation in a standard:

  > "Let's talk about task handovers. What good looks like, what we've seen, and what we want to reinforce."

- **Afternoon – Growth Conversation (25 min)**
  Check in with a future team leader or someone with growth potential. Ask:

  "What's something you're still figuring out as a leader?"

Thursday

- **Morning – System Check (25 min)**
  Choose one recurring breakdown. Map it with the coachee:

  "Where's the friction point? How could we shift that upstream?"
  This is coaching the system, not just the individual.

- **End-of-day – Pattern Reflection (15 min)**
  Ask:

  "What habits are starting to form in the team—and are they serving us?"

Friday

- **Weekly Close-Out & Coaching Recap (30 min)**
  Walk the floor. Recognise someone's improvement. Share what was done well publicly.

- **Personal Leadership Debrief (15 min)**
  Ask yourself:

  "Who did I develop this week? What landed? What didn't? What do I need to adjust?"
  This is where your own coaching habits grow.

What's the Point?

A good week isn't one where you put out all the fires. **It's one where you built capability so fewer fires start.**

This cadence is not rigid—it flexes with the demands of the work—but it provides a leadership scaffold that signals to your team that development is ongoing, not optional. It balances the realities of real-time performance with the commitment to long-term growth. It tells the story of your leadership not through strategy documents or meeting minutes, but through consistent presence. You do not need to coach all the time; you need to coach every time it matters. And the only way to ensure that happens is to plan for it. Coaching does not scale because of good intentions—it scales because of rhythm. And rhythm is what makes leadership visible, not just to others, but to yourself.

In this chapter, we reframed coaching not as a reactive task, but as **a systemised leadership behaviour**. A leadership discipline that requires protection, structure, and repetition—just like safety, production, or quality.

You learned that:

- **Good intentions don't create consistency**—structure does. When coaching isn't in your calendar, it's not in your leadership.

- **Leader Standard Work** is how coaching becomes a habit. It moves coaching from the "urgent pile" to the "identity pile."

- The **Three Calendar Buckets** model helps you manage coaching as part of your role—not as a bonus. Role-critical, flexible, and growth work all have a place if you design for them.

- A **Protected Coaching Window** isn't a luxury—it's a leadership cue. What you protect signals what you prioritise. When others see you guard that time, they treat coaching as real.

- And finally, **a good coaching week isn't crammed—it's intentional.** A rhythm of presence, curiosity, development, and accountability that unfolds visibly and sustainably across time.

The shift here is more than just a change in mindset—it's a transformation in how leadership is practised and perceived:

From coaching as an event → to coaching as a leadership function.
From scattered efforts → to repeatable patterns.
From aspiration → to operational identity.

If your calendar doesn't reflect a consistent coaching rhythm, your team's behaviour won't reflect one either. Leadership habits are not just taught—they are modelled. When coaching is visible, scheduled, and repeated week after week, it stops being a standalone act. It becomes part of how the team learns, adapts, and delivers. That is the rhythm of real leadership. And like all powerful rhythms, it does not begin by accident—it begins by design.

PART 4:

WHEN GROWTH OUTLIVES YOU

Chapter 13:

The Signals of Real Progress

There's a common belief among seasoned leaders: "I know if someone's improving—I can feel it." That instinct, built over years in the field, is often right. But it's also incomplete.

Gut feel gives you a signal. But it doesn't give you a system. And if there's one thing we've learned in this book, it's that what's not systematised doesn't scale. The challenge with relying on instinct alone is that it can be biased, reactive, and difficult to explain. What one leader calls "potential," another may overlook entirely. What feels like progress on a good day might feel like slippage on a stressful one. And when someone asks, "How do you know your team is growing?"—a shrug or a feeling isn't good enough.

This is where **growth indicators** come in. They help you move from coaching as an experience to coaching as an outcome. From something you do to something you can see. And not just you—the coachee too.

These indicators aren't complicated. They're simple, visible signs that your coaching is landing. Signs like:

- A team member self-correcting without needing to be reminded.

- A shift in language: from "I was told" to "I decided."

- A supervisor reflecting on their influence, not just their task.

- A crew running the safety prep conversation without prompting.

- A previously quiet operator speaking up about a process gap.

Each of these is a data point. A behavioural feedback loop. A **signal that belief is turning into ownership**. And when you start tracking these signals—not obsessively, but intentionally—you begin to build confidence that what you're doing matters. That coaching isn't just a conversation. It's a catalyst. Leaders often ask, "How do I know if it's working?"

The answer is simple: **you start seeing your coaching show up when you're not in the room.** That's the ultimate growth indicator. Not better answers while you're present—

but better decisions when you're not.

When leaders want to track progress, the instinct is often to zoom in—to inspect more closely, analyse more data, ask more follow-up questions. But that instinct, while well-meaning, can drift quickly into micromanagement. And micromanagement doesn't build capability. It builds compliance and resentment.

That's why great leaders don't use a magnifying glass. They use a mirror. A magnifying glass inspects. A mirror reflects. Magnifying lenses are used to spot errors. Mirrors are used to help people see themselves. In coaching, this distinction is crucial. If your intent is to build independent thinkers—people who can self-correct, self-assess, and self-lead—then they need a **clear reflection of their own behaviours**, not just your analysis of it.And this is exactly where reflective coaching becomes your best tool.

When a team member walks away from a coaching session saying, "I know what I did well, I know where I fell short, and I know what I'm going to do differently"—that's evidence of growth. Not because you told them, but because they saw it for themselves.

You can't always be there to direct every action. But you can build people who think, adapt, and reflect—without needing a nudge. That's what the mirror creates: **internal feedback loops** that keep growing long after the conversation ends. Research on self-regulated learning and leadership development confirms that reflective practices—especially when supported by timely coaching—strengthen metacognition, foster adaptive thinking, and reinforce autonomous problem-solving [20].

The most powerful thing a leader can give someone isn't more instructions.
It's **the ability to see clearly—on their own**. This is also how you track growth without tracking everything. You don't need a dashboard for every detail. You need to ask: Are they starting to reflect the coaching back to me? Are they seeing what I used to have to point out? Are their questions becoming deeper, more proactive, more aware?

That's the mirror in action. It doesn't magnify flaws. It illuminates progress.

And in leadership, that's what you're trying to grow—not perfect performers, but self-aware, self-improving people who don't need constant correction to get better. Tracking growth without micromanaging isn't just a leadership mindset—it's a practice. It means building feedback loops that allow you to **see capability progress over time**, without overreaching or reducing people to performance checklists. The solution lies in tools that are **light enough to use regularly**, but **robust enough to show patterns**. And that's where coaching journals, development logs, and simple dashboards come in. Not as bureaucratic add-ons, but as visible thinking spaces—for you, and for your team.

Coaching Journals (for the leader)

Think of a coaching journal as your personal field record—a space where you document key coaching interactions, emerging behaviours, and themes you want to revisit. It isn't a report. It's your **leadership memory**.

Why it works:

- You capture what was said, seen, or surfaced in the moment.

- You begin to notice trends: Is someone consistently avoiding risk conversations? Has someone started reinforcing standards to others?

- You reduce guesswork: Instead of "I think we had that conversation," you have a record that shows how development unfolded.

You can use a physical notebook, a digital log, or even voice notes transcribed after each session. Format is flexible. What matters is that you're **reflecting on your own coaching impact**, not just ticking boxes.

And over time, this becomes your coaching story. It gives you examples to reinforce, moments to return to, and **evidence that your leadership is moving people forward.**

Development Logs (for the coachee)

While your coaching journal helps you track insights, a **development log** belongs to your team. This is a simple reflection tool you give to the coachee—prompted by a few intentional questions:

- What did you learn this week?

- What habit did you practice?

- Where did you face a challenge, and how did you respond?

- What's one shift you want to carry into next week?

You're not auditing this. You're **encouraging ownership**.

Used well, a development log becomes a mirror they carry with them—making it easier for them to connect the dots between what they do, what they learn, and how they grow. It builds metacognition and quiet discipline. It builds self-leadership.

Simple Dashboards (for visibility)

Dashboards don't need to be technical. You don't need software. You need a way to **visualise growth at a glance**. For example:

- A whiteboard or spreadsheet where you track which crew members received formal coaching this week.

- Colour-coded notes beside names: Red (needs focus), Yellow (developing), Green (self-leading).

- A monthly snapshot: What behaviours are improving? What standards are slipping? What conversations need repeating?

Used well, these tools create **leadership visibility without surveillance**. They make your team's development tangible—so you can speak to it with clarity. And they help you avoid uneven focus, favouritism, or blind spots.

This is especially important when you're managing multiple crews, shifts, or leaders. You can't remember every detail—but you can track the right patterns.

What Makes These Tools Powerful?

1. **They make coaching visible.**
   Development is no longer anecdotal—it's observable, referenceable, and continuous.

2. **They build habits.**
   When journaling and reflection become routine, growth becomes part of how the team operates—not something they wait for you to deliver.

3. **They depersonalise correction.**
   You can show someone a pattern in their own words or reflections, not just your critique. It makes feedback easier to receive and more likely to stick.

4. **They create leadership calm.**
   Instead of scrambling to remember what you said last week, you've got a record. That frees your mind to focus on the next layer of coaching—not just the surface tasks.

The point of all these tools is simple: **Track the growth, not the person.**
When coaching becomes a structured rhythm—reinforced by light, consistent tracking tools—you no longer need to chase performance. You're now curating a development story. One with evidence, insight, and momentum. Because in the end, leadership isn't just about action. It's about **making learning visible**.

If you want people to grow, you have to show them they're growing. Not with generic praise. Not with "good job" handshakes. But with **specific recognition** of what's improving—and why it matters. Because what you celebrate, people repeat. And what gets acknowledged, gets anchored. In a performance-driven culture, it's easy to fixate on what's still broken. Leaders see the gaps, the slips, the near misses. But what often gets missed are the small signals that say, "It's starting to land." That's where belief builds. That's where confidence grows. And that's where sustainable change begins.

Celebrating small wins isn't soft. It's strategic. Especially in a coaching system where growth happens gradually, not all at once.

What Do Small Wins Look Like?

In frontline coaching, small wins are often behavioural. They show up in moments that don't always make the daily report, but fundamentally shift how a person works, thinks, or shows up.

Examples:

- A team member stops before a task and says, "Let's check if we've covered all the controls."

- A quiet operator offers a peer some advice on standard procedure—with confidence.

- A supervisor corrects a task gap with calm, fact-based feedback—mirroring the exact coaching tone you've modelled.

- Someone who used to wait for permission starts raising improvement ideas without prompting.

- A crew member reflects, mid-task, "We missed that last time—let's not do it again."

These are not random. These are **evidence of internalised coaching**.

And when you name them—clearly, visibly, and publicly—you reinforce not just the behaviour, but the belief behind it.

Why Milestone Recognition Matters

Growth is not always linear. People have setbacks. Progress is messy. That's why you need milestone markers—**signals of advancement** that remind individuals: you're on the right track, even if you haven't arrived yet.

Think of it like scaffolding: if you want people to climb higher, you have to secure the level they're standing on. Celebrating a development milestone is how you do that.

For example:

- When a new team leader runs their first coaching huddle independently, acknowledge it.

- When a team shifts from needing direction to offering self-reflection, call it out.

- When a peer-to-peer standard check replaces a top-down reminder, frame it as progress.

These aren't trophies. They're **leadership cues**. They tell people:

> "This is the behaviour we want more of. You're doing it. Keep going."

And they tell the team:

> "Growth here is possible, visible, and real."

How to Celebrate Without Creating Dependence

Leaders sometimes worry that praise will create performance dependency. That people will start performing for the pat on the back. But effective coaching doesn't celebrate compliance. It celebrates **ownership.**

So your recognition must be:

- **Specific**: "I saw how you stopped the team to check the barricade. That's a real sign of ownership."

- **Anchored**: "That's exactly what good looks like. It's aligned to our safety coaching standard."

- **Forward-pointing**: "Keep applying that mindset across the whole task set—you're clearly building leadership depth."

The goal of recognition in coaching is not to create reward-chasers. It's not about praise for its own sake. The aim is to mirror progress back to the individual—so they can see it, feel it, and replicate it with intention. When a person begins to recognise their own growth, reinforcement becomes internal. And that's how coaching stops being an event and starts becoming culture.

Celebrating as a Growth Loop

When you coach, track, and celebrate—even in small ways—you create a growth loop:

1. **Insight** from coaching leads to

2. **Action** by the coachee, which produces

3. **Evidence** of growth that gets

4. **Reinforced** through recognition, encouraging

5. **More reflection and deeper ownership**—starting the loop again.

This loop sustains belief. And belief sustains performance. So the next time you see a small shift—name it. Reinforce it. Let them hear it. Let others see it.Because when you treat small wins like milestones, you teach your team that growth is happening—even when it's hard to see. One of the greatest truths about coaching is also one of the hardest for leaders to trust: **it works even when you can't see it right away**.

Coaching is like compound interest. The early returns feel small. Progress is subtle. But over time, the gains multiply. The conversations you had last month start to show up in someone's decisions today. The standard you modelled last quarter becomes the norm in next quarter's team meetings. The mindset shift you planted on a Tuesday becomes the reason a mistake is avoided three weeks later. This is the **compound effect of coaching**—slow at first, then suddenly visible everywhere. But to recognise this kind of growth, leaders need a different lens. Not the lens of instant feedback, but the lens of **accumulated influence**.

What Does Compounded Growth Look Like?

It's rarely loud. Often, it doesn't announce itself. But here's how you know your coaching is starting to compound:

- A supervisor you've coached for months begins coaching others—using your language, tone, and method.

- A team that used to need reminders now starts meetings by reflecting on last week's performance.

- A peer steps in to reinforce a standard—not because they were asked, but because they've internalised its value.

- A near-miss is caught and corrected—not by the leader, but by the crew themselves.

- A first-time leader says, "I coached it the way you coached me."

These aren't one-off wins. They're signs that **coaching has entered the bloodstream** of the team. And they're only visible if you're looking for them—if you've trained your eye not just on the outcome, but on the **evolution of thinking and behaviour** over time. Coaching doesn't just shape performance—it shapes belief. And belief is what people fall back on when conditions get tough.

When your coaching compounds:

- You don't need to be present to maintain standards.

- Your team starts solving problems before they escalate.

- Confidence builds—not just in individuals, but in the crew as a unit.

- You're not managing every moment—you're guiding the system.

This is what real leadership looks like: **less control, more influence**. Not because you let go—but because you built something that lasts beyond you. This kind of growth won't show up on a dashboard. But it will show up in patterns. Here's what to listen for and notice:

- Language shifts: "We" statements replace "they" statements. Standards are referenced voluntarily.

- Decision logic: People start explaining why they did something in terms that mirror your coaching approach.

- Cultural traction: New starters are coached by peers—not just trained on tasks, but inducted into thinking.

- Peer accountability: A frontline operator corrects another—not from ego, but from shared belief.

- Behavioural depth: Someone doesn't just complete a task—they **anticipate** risk, improve process, and teach others.

These are the signs that coaching is no longer something you do.

It's something the team has learned to do **within themselves and for each other.**

When You See It, Say It.When you notice the compound effect kicking in, name it.Say: "That's exactly what we talked about two months ago. You're applying it without even realising."
 Say: "I saw how you coached your peer the way we've practised—solid work."
 Say: "This culture you're building—this is what real leadership looks like."

Because once your team realises that change isn't luck—that it's built on repeated action and reflection—they start to trust the process. And they start to lead the process. That's how coaching becomes culture. Not overnight. Not from powerful conversation but from a **compound rhythm** of belief, action, feedback, and trust—over time.

Chapter 14:

When Habits Turn Into Culture

When Repetition Becomes Identity

Culture doesn't start with intention—it starts with repetition. Not the once-off motivational moment, not the formal training rollout, but the quiet, unglamorous act of doing something important again and again until it no longer feels optional. As a frontline leader, you don't create culture by talking about it. You create it by repeating the right behaviours until the team stops seeing them as yours—and starts seeing them as *ours*.

One of the most powerful coaching habits you can build is rhythm. Whether it's ending the shift with a single reflective question, opening toolbox meetings with a mindset check, or pausing after errors to coach before correcting—it's the repetition that makes the difference. The first time you do it, they notice. The fifth time, they expect it. The fiftieth time, *they do it without you.*

Repetition is what forms behavioural memory. The team starts to anticipate what comes next. After the shift? "He's going to ask us what we learned." After a tough moment? "She's probably going to ask what we would do differently next time." And once that groove is laid, it no longer needs a reminder. The habit becomes an internal rhythm—and that rhythm starts to guide performance.

In the early days, coaching habits often look like compliance. People copy what they see because they think they have to. But when you stay consistent—calmly, deliberately—that habit begins to change shape. It transforms from something people perform *for you* to something they begin to do *for themselves*. That shift—from compliance to confidence—is where identity is formed. And identity is where culture begins.

You'll know you've crossed the threshold when the environment starts carrying the habit. Maybe there's a visual check-in board where people write their own daily learning. Maybe someone sets up the coaching prompt before you arrive. Maybe the peer next to them says, "Let's reflect before we rush it." That's not just a behaviour. That's culture speaking through your team.

Repetition also builds trust. When a coaching moment happens at the same time, in the same way, for the same reason—it becomes predictable. And predictability builds psychological safety. People begin to believe, *"This isn't a one-off. This is who we are now."* The habit becomes reliable. And when it's reliable, it becomes internalised.

Most telling of all is how people behave under pressure. When everything is going wrong and time is tight—*what do they default to?* That default is your culture. If they reflect before reacting, ask a better question, coach each other instead of blaming—that's not instinct. That's identity formed through repetition.

So keep repeating the right habits, even when it feels like no one's watching. Because someone is. And eventually, *everyone* will be.

> **Insight:**
> *When coaching becomes a reflex, culture becomes a mirror.*

What You Say, They Start to Say

Culture often finds its voice in language—long before it shows up in metrics. As a frontline leader, what you say repeatedly starts to shape how your team thinks, how they respond, and how they lead. Over time, your coaching phrases become cultural code: small, familiar scripts that shape big behavioural shifts.

You might not realise it at first. You'll say something like, *"What's your next move?"* at the end of a shift. Or you'll pause after an error and ask, *"What would you do differently if this happened again?"* These questions aren't magic. But when used consistently, they start to reshape how your team processes experience. The words become normal. Then they become expected. Eventually, they become theirs.

This is where coaching turns into culture. When the same language is used over and over, it creates shared mental models. People begin to know what matters—because they've heard it named enough times. Language consistency builds emotional safety too. If feedback is always framed the same way—calm, curious, without judgement—people stop bracing for blame. They start leaning into growth.

You'll know the shift is happening when your words start coming back to you—from other mouths. A team member asks a peer, *"What did you learn from that?"* Someone says during a meeting, *"Let's reflect before we jump in."* They're not copying to impress you. They're speaking in the language that now defines how your team works. It's no longer *your* coaching voice. It's the team's shared language.

That shared language is also a signal of shared mindset. When multiple people are using the same questions, prompts, or coaching cues, it means the beliefs underneath the words are taking hold. The team isn't just echoing—they're aligned. That's how you know it's becoming cultural: when your phrases aren't just spoken, they're *believed*.

And in high-pressure moments, language becomes even more powerful. When things go wrong, most teams default to silence or reaction. But a coaching culture has a script. A way of naming what's happening, reflecting quickly, and deciding wisely. That doesn't happen by accident—it happens because the language was practiced when the pressure was low.

So keep repeating the words that shape how your team sees itself. Speak coaching into every shift. Not because you're trying to train parrots—but because you're building the vocabulary of belief.

> **Insight:**
> *Habits shape how we speak—language shapes how we lead.*

Cadence Turns Practice Into Pattern

It's not what we do once that shapes the team. It's what we do **every time**. Rhythm, more than any other habit, is what turns leadership into memory. When something happens predictably—at the same time, in the same way—it begins to feel natural. That's what builds cultural memory: the sense that, *"This is just how we do things here."*

Leaders often overestimate the impact of intensity and underestimate the power of consistency. One powerful coaching conversation may spark a shift—but it's rhythm that sustains it. When a habit like reflection or feedback happens on a consistent cadence, it stops feeling like a leadership initiative and starts feeling like normal life.

Think of it this way: if every Monday starts with a coaching prompt, or every Friday ends with a team reflection, your people start to anticipate the moment before it happens. That anticipation builds readiness. It reduces friction. And it reinforces the message: "This isn't just something we do—it's part of our operating rhythm."

That rhythm also creates psychological safety. Predictability helps people show up fully prepared. They don't brace for a surprise review or unexpected coaching—they lean into the routine. The structure itself becomes supportive. It tells people what to expect, when to prepare, and how to participate. It lowers the emotional cost of growth.

Over time, these repetitive moments create time-anchored memory. "This is what we always do on Thursdays." "We always check in at the start of a shift." The rhythm becomes cultural scaffolding. People stop wondering if it's happening and start planning around it. And because it happens reliably, it feels real. Not imposed. Not artificial. Just real.

But when the rhythm breaks—when coaching stops, reviews get skipped, or reflection disappears—the culture notices. The message becomes blurry. "Maybe this wasn't as important as we thought." And in that space, inconsistency creeps in. That's why leadership rhythm isn't about the leader's calendar. It's about the team's memory.

So if you want your habits to stick, give them rhythm. Repeat the things that matter. Anchor them to time, place, or ritual. Because rhythm doesn't just create routine—it builds retention. It keeps the culture alive, even when things get messy.

> **Closing insight:**
> *Rhythm isn't routine—it's retention.*

You Get More of What You Celebrate

Most coaching cultures aren't built on big speeches. They're built on **small acknowledgements**—moments when a leader sees something worth reinforcing, names it, and lets the team know, *"That matters here."* The habit of noticing is subtle. But over time, it becomes one of the most powerful cultural levers a frontline leader can use.

You don't need a formal reward system to shift a team's behaviour. You just need a sharp eye and a repeatable habit of recognition. When someone pauses to reflect before reacting—and you name it? That's reinforcement. When a team member gives feedback constructively—and you spotlight it? That's confirmation. In a high-speed environment, people remember what gets noticed more than what gets assigned.

These moments don't have to be dramatic. In fact, the smaller and more specific the reinforcement, the stronger the cultural effect. "You stepped back and asked a great coaching question." "You gave that feedback clearly but respectfully." When leaders recognise *the belief behind the behaviour*, they're reinforcing more than an outcome—they're reinforcing identity.

Naming good habits also builds shared language. Once a behaviour is recognised, it becomes something others can reference. "That's what it looks like when we coach each other," becomes part of the team's mental model. It gives people examples they can follow—real moments from within their own group.

And when that recognition happens in front of others, it amplifies the effect. Public reinforcement doesn't just affirm the individual—it teaches the team what matters. People take note. They remember. And they begin to emulate. The loop is simple: what's seen gets named, what's named gets repeated, and what's repeated becomes culture.

But there's a catch: if good habits aren't noticed, they often fade. When people take a risk to do something differently—pause, reflect, coach a peer—and no one acknowledges it, they assume it didn't matter. Over time, those small acts vanish. That's why noticing isn't just a feel-good gesture. It's a leadership responsibility.

So make it a habit. Catch people doing it right. Name the micro-wins. Reflect belief back to the team before they ask for it. Because what you notice becomes what they value. And what they value becomes the way they lead.

> **Insight:**
> *Noticing is the habit that builds belief.*

From Leader-Coached to Peer-Coached

At first, coaching is something you do *for* your team. You initiate the conversation. You ask the questions. You guide the reflection. But over time, if the habit is consistent and the tone is right, something remarkable begins to happen. Coaching stops being a *leader's job*—and starts becoming *everyone's responsibility*.

The first signal is self-direction. A team member pauses after a mistake and says, *"Let me take a minute to figure out what I'd do differently."* No prompt. No pressure. Just reflection. That's not coincidence—it's cultural uptake. What began as something externally modelled is now internally owned. They're coaching themselves.

Then, you start to see it peer-to-peer. One operator offers another a suggestion—calm, specific, grounded in belief. "Hey, I noticed that didn't land—want to talk it through?" That's coaching. And it's not top-down. It's cultural. When feedback travels sideways, it means the habit has transferred. And when it transfers, it multiplies.

At this point, you're no longer the only signal. The team begins to carry the habit forward. Others remind each other to reflect before reacting. Standards are upheld even in your absence. The coaching tone you once introduced is now being protected by the team itself. That's the essence of a culture shift: behaviour that no longer requires your constant presence to survive.

What used to be "impressive" becomes "normal." The team doesn't wait for feedback—they expect it. They don't avoid reflective questions—they ask them first. Coaching has moved from being something special to being something shared. And when coaching becomes common, high performance becomes sustainable.

This cultural maturity isn't just about performance—it's about resilience. A team that coaches itself can recover faster, solve problems more creatively, and adapt without relying on the leader to carry every issue. It becomes a system, not a series of isolated conversations.

So keep coaching—but watch for the signs that your team is starting to coach without you. When that happens, you're not just growing individuals. You're building a culture that doesn't need pushing. It pulls itself forward.

Insight:
When everyone becomes a coach, culture becomes self-sustaining.

New People Experience Your Culture, Not Your Words

Culture isn't defined by your most experienced team members—it's revealed in how your *newest* ones are treated. Every new hire steps into your leadership system like a blank page. And what they see, hear, and absorb in their first days tells them exactly what kind of team they've joined. Not because of the welcome speech—but because of the habits that show up without needing to be explained.

You don't build culture during onboarding. You **reveal it**. If a new starter arrives and sees daily reflection, peer coaching, and calm correction happening as part of the rhythm—they'll adopt it without question. Not because it was taught in a manual, but because it was modelled from day one. Habits are contagious, and new people are highly susceptible.

This is why the first week matters more than any induction pack. Onboarding is a cultural echo chamber. Whatever habits you've embedded—good or bad—get amplified. If the team reflects after each shift, gives feedback respectfully, and uses coaching language naturally, the new hire will start copying it without even realising. They're not being trained. They're being imprinted.

Early exposure to coaching is critical. If new hires are coached early—*not just trained*—they adapt faster. They're not just learning tasks. They're learning tone. They understand that reflection, not reaction, is how we do things here. That standards are real because they're upheld in rhythm, not just written down.

But here's the trap: if onboarding is outsourced—left to HR or delegated to someone who doesn't model the same habits—then cultural transfer breaks. The leader must remain close enough to shape the tone, at least in the beginning. Because culture doesn't scale through process. It scales through proximity.

And perhaps most revealing of all: **every new hire is a mirror**. How quickly they absorb your habits—and how they behave in week two—reflects the clarity of your coaching culture. If they begin reflecting without prompting, asking better questions, or coaching others quickly, you'll know your habits are alive. If they default to silence, shortcuts, or confusion, you'll know where your system is leaking.

So treat onboarding like a leadership test. Not of the person joining—but of the system they're entering. What do they see repeated? What do they absorb without being told? That's your culture—raw and visible.

> **Insight:**
> *Culture isn't what you say to new starters—it's what they see repeated.*

Look Back to Grow Forward

The strongest teams don't just act—they reflect. They build a rhythm of looking back, not out of guilt or blame, but because growth demands awareness. As a frontline leader, one of the most sustainable habits you can build is **team reflection**. And when that habit repeats, it becomes more than a review—it becomes your culture's internal compass.

At first, reflection starts with you. You ask the questions. You hold space at the end of the shift. You bring the team together after a tough job and say, *"What worked? What didn't? What would we do differently next time?"* It might feel forced at first. But if you stay consistent, it becomes familiar. Then expected. Then owned.

Over time, you'll notice something shift: reflection starts happening without you. Someone else asks the question. A team member calls for a debrief. Or someone stops the group midstream and says, *"Let's take a step back before we carry on."* That's the mark of cultural maturity—when reflection becomes a team reflex, not just a leader's routine.

Shared reflection changes how the team understands success. It's no longer just about hitting targets—it's about learning how they got there. It reduces ego and increases ownership. It builds emotional honesty and collective confidence. Instead of finger-pointing, the team asks better questions. Instead of defensiveness, there's curiosity.

It also prevents coaching fatigue. When reflection becomes a group rhythm, the leader doesn't have to push every growth moment. The team starts adjusting on its own. That means fewer course corrections from you—and more course-setting by them. Reflection lightens your leadership load because it distributes responsibility for learning.

And it protects your culture. Habits can drift over time. Standards soften. Shortcuts sneak in. But reflection brings things back into focus. Weekly, even daily, moments to pause, ask, realign, and recommit keep the culture fresh. Not through control—but through conversation.

A reflective team is not just high-performing. It's **self-correcting**. And that's the ultimate mark of cultural strength: not needing perfect leadership, but having a shared way of growing—even when no one is watching.

> **Insight:**
> *When reflection becomes rhythmic, growth becomes automatic.*

The Culture Is the Proof

Culture doesn't arrive with a strategy. It doesn't come from a rollout. It doesn't need a banner or a branding session. Culture emerges quietly—through the things you repeat, the tone you set, and the habits you protect even when no one's checking.

That's what this chapter has really been about. The moment where coaching stops being something *you do* and starts becoming something *they become*. When repetition turns into identity. When your language becomes theirs. When rhythm builds memory, and noticing builds belief. When reflection becomes the way your team resets, grows, and moves forward—without waiting for your lead.

You won't always see the shift when it happens. There's no big flag. No announcement. Just a quieter day. A solved problem. A conversation between two team members that sounds a lot like the ones you used to lead. And that's the point. When coaching becomes the culture, your leadership doesn't disappear—it multiplies.

This is how real empowerment works. Not through delegation alone, but through habit transfer. Through shared language, shared rhythm, shared reflection. Through systems of belief that your team begins to carry for themselves.

So if you're wondering whether your coaching is working—stop looking at the scoreboard. Start listening to your team. Hear the tone. Watch the repetition. Pay attention to what continues even when you're not there.

Because when your habits become theirs, you're not just building better performers—you're building a culture that coaches itself. When coaching is consistent and growth is visible, you don't just develop stronger individuals; you create a team that can coach itself. In the end, culture becomes the loudest proof of your quietest habits.

Chapter 15:

The Spiral of Legacy

Somewhere along the way, many of us inherited the belief that leadership is something you arrive at. A position. A title. A milestone that says, "You've made it." But real leadership doesn't arrive. It returns.

It loops back with more clarity. It widens its view. It deepens its practice. And just when you think you've mastered something, the context changes—and you're invited to begin again, but this time with more wisdom. That's the rhythm of coaching leadership. Not a straight line. A spiral. One that moves from intention to action, from insight to impact, and then back to intention—each cycle refining who you are and how you lead.

If you've made it this far in the book, it means something important: you've chosen a path that few take. Not the path of position—but the path of practice. The kind of leadership that gets its hands dirty. That notices. That reflects. That grows alongside the team. But here's the truth you need to carry now: this path doesn't end here. There is no final level. There's only the next layer.

The next time you coach someone through a challenge you once faced.
The next moment you pause, reflect, and respond instead of react.
The next standard you reinforce—not because the business asked you to, but because you believe it matters.

That's what mastery looks like. Not perfection.
Just presence. Repeated. Refined. Recommitted.

Leadership at the frontline is not a static achievement. It's a dynamic identity—one that grows as you grow. One that requires rhythm, not rank. Curiosity, not certainty. And the humility to know that who you are becoming is just as important as what you deliver. This isn't the end of your journey. It's the deepening of it. There comes a moment in every leader's journey when the shift happens. The shift from driving results to developing people. From executing the plan to enabling others to lead the plan. From being the centre of the system to building a system that works without you.

Legacy in frontline leadership isn't built through charisma. It's built through **capability transfer**—when the thinking, standard, tone, and rhythm you've modelled starts to replicate in others. When your team stops waiting for you and starts anticipating what good looks like. When they coach each other, hold each other to standard, and course-correct without fear or favour—because they believe in what they're upholding.

That's not compliance. That's **empowerment.**

You'll know it's taking root when people around you stop asking for answers and start seeking clarity. When they say, "I've thought about this and here's what I propose." When they offer feedback to each other the same way you once offered it to them. When they reflect—out loud—before you even ask the question.

It doesn't happen overnight. But it does happen—when you coach with belief, and when you reinforce what matters without needing to be the loudest voice in the room.

Your legacy isn't the shift you led or the project you delivered—it's the mindset and method you leave behind. It's whether your team can continue leading in your absence, whether the standards remain high when no one is watching, and whether your rhythm of coaching becomes theirs. Leadership studies increasingly highlight that the most enduring form of legacy is not authority, but capability—embedded through systems, modelled in practice, and owned collectively. When coaching becomes part of the team's own rhythm, empowerment shifts from idea to identity [21].

Empowerment is not just about giving responsibility—it's about building readiness through clarity, practice, trust, and rhythm. When you invest in that kind of leadership, your impact outlives your presence. That's legacy. Not a name on a wall, but a belief system embedded in people. Not a role remembered, but a way of working that remains. And the beauty is, it starts in quiet moments—a question asked, a reflection held, a belief reinforced. That's how culture shifts. That's how leaders multiply. That's how you leave something that lasts.

There's a reason we place so much emphasis on reflection in coaching: it's not just a learning tool—it's a survival trait. In a world where conditions shift daily—where teams face turnover, uncertainty, and sudden change—reflection is how leaders regain perspective without losing presence. It allows them to process what happened, extract meaning from the mess, and recalibrate without collapsing under the weight of the unknown. Adaptation begins here—not with new instructions or better forecasts, but with a leader who pauses long enough to ask:

> "What changed, and what does it ask of me now?"

Coaching builds this habit into your system. It teaches your people to stop, notice, and name what's shifted—internally and externally. And it teaches you, the leader, to model **responsive calm**, even when the environment is far from calm.

This is resilience—not the absence of stress, but the ability to bend without breaking, to learn amid challenge, to stay anchored when expectations shift, and to adapt without losing your standard. And this is where coaching becomes more than a skill—it becomes a stabilising force. When systems change, leadership gaps widen. People feel uncertain. Direction becomes unclear. But the leaders who have embedded reflective practice—who coach not just to correct but to equip—are the ones who hold the line. Not with rigidity, but with rhythm. Not with panic, but with presence..

They ask questions like:

- What's still true in this moment?

- What does good look like now?

- Where's the opportunity—not just the loss?

- What can we reinforce, even when everything else is shifting?

When you coach with these questions—especially in uncertainty—you're doing more than supporting. You're shaping how your team responds to pressure. You're building psychological flexibility. You're showing that resilience is not luck. It's practiced reflection, repeated adaptation, and consistent reinforcement of what matters most.

That is the kind of leadership that does not merely survive change—it grows stronger because of it. Leadership is often imagined as a ladder: something to climb, rung by rung, until one reaches a higher vantage point—confident, elevated, and complete. But coaching teaches us something different. Leadership is not linear. It is not a set of steps to ascend and then leave behind. Instead, it is a spiral—a recurring rhythm that deepens with each cycle and strengthens through repetition.

Every time you coach someone, you return to the same three anchors:

1. You **set** the standard—clear, visible, and reinforced.

2. You **monitor** performance—not to judge, but to understand.

3. You **coach**—to close the gap between what is and what could be.

Then it begins again.

You revisit that same process the next shift, the next week, the next change initiative. But you're not repeating in place. You're spiraling upward. You're bringing more experience, more trust, more insight into every cycle. The pattern stays familiar. But your influence grows deeper. Your questions land faster. Your team responds earlier.

That's the spiral of mastery.
Same rhythm. Deeper layers.

This spiral is also what protects leaders from burnout and disillusionment. It offers the perspective that you are not starting over each time someone forgets a step or misses a cue. You are not failing—you are in the spiral. You are reinforcing, repeating, and refining. You are investing in the next layer of leadership. When your team begins to mirror that spiral—setting their own standards, monitoring themselves, and coaching one another—you know the system is taking root. You are no longer the sole driver of improvement. The rhythm has transferred. The spiral has widened. This is how culture changes: not through isolated events, but through repeated behaviours, consistently layered with intent..

So as you look forward, don't ask, "What comes next?"
Ask, "What layer are we deepening now?"

Leadership is not about climbing. It is about cycling back through the work that matters most—each time with greater clarity, deeper courage, and steadier calm. Every leader eventually leaves their post. The role will be filled by someone else. The title will be passed on. The task list will be reassigned. But what endures is not the position you held—it is the mindset and method you left behind..

What remains—what truly lasts—is the mark you leave on people. Not the performance reviews or project dashboards, but the rhythms you taught, the beliefs you modelled, and the conversations that reshaped how others saw themselves. That is the real test of leadership: can they still feel your coaching when you are no longer there? If you have coached with consistency—reinforcing standards without blame, building ownership without fear, and developing capability without control—then your departure will not leave a gap; it will reveal a strength. It will uncover what was always there, embedded by your presence and now carried by the system. And if you have built that system—if your team knows how to reflect, review, reinforce, and respond—then you have done more than your job. You have left a way of working that others can inherit. That is what it means to leave a mark.

This book does not end with a list or a slogan. It ends where your leadership continues—in the conversations you hold, the habits you reinforce, and the belief you choose to build in others every single day. The ideas shared here were never meant to be memorised like rules. They were meant to shape how you think, how you show up, and how you lead when no one is watching.

Because real leadership does not announce itself. It becomes visible through repetition—through the way people grow under your guidance, not your control. Through the way teams begin to expect more from themselves because you expected more from them, and held that expectation with steadiness and care. Through the way your rhythm becomes theirs, and your questions become part of how they think.

The habits you've nurtured, the standards you've coached, and the clarity you've provided will outlast your role, your presence, even your name. That is the quiet truth of coaching: its impact is not always immediate, but it is always multiplying. Long after you've stepped back, the mindset you modelled will still echo in how people lead, how they solve problems, how they hold each other to account—not because they were told to, but because they were taught how.

And that is the mark of real leadership. It does not seek visibility. It seeks continuity. It does not depend on power. It depends on presence. It does not try to own the outcome. It invests in the people who will shape it.

If you've stayed with this book to the end, then you already understand something essential: frontline coaching is not a task to complete or a technique to master. It is a language. And like all meaningful languages, it reveals what we truly believe. When you speak as a coach, you are not just communicating instructions. You are signaling belief. You are making it clear that the person in front of you is capable of growth, worthy of responsibility, and trusted to lead.

This is what empowerment really means. It is not praise without substance, nor kindness without clarity. It is the deliberate act of equipping someone to operate without your constant oversight. It is the confidence to let others think, decide, and take ownership—because you have made the standard clear, the feedback consistent, and the rhythm strong enough to hold even when you're not in the room.

That is why coaching matters. Not because it improves performance in the moment, although it does. But because it builds the muscle of leadership in others. It creates self-correcting systems, self-accountable teams, and individuals who know how to lead from wherever they stand. And that kind of impact cannot be achieved through pressure. It only comes through presence.

So as this final chapter closes, recognise what it leaves open. You have not just finished reading a book. You have sharpened the lens through which you lead. You have built new language for conversations that matter. You have taken a step toward the kind of leadership that scales—not through control, but through clarity. Not through charisma, but through cadence. Not through your position, but through the habits you've chosen to practice and pass on.

And that is how leadership becomes a system. That is how it lasts. That is how it spreads—quietly, steadily, through the daily decisions of leaders like you who choose to make belief visible, and coaching real. You've done more than improve a process. You've grown people. And in doing so, you've built something far more enduring than performance. You've built a legacy.

References

[1] Edmondson, A.C. (2019). *The Fearless Organization: Creating Psychological Safety in the Workplace for Learning, Innovation, and Growth*. Hoboken, NJ: Wiley.

[2] Katzenbach, J.R., & Smith, D.K. (2005). *The Wisdom of Teams: Creating the High-Performance Organization*. New York: Harper Business.

[3] Lencioni, P. (2002). *The Five Dysfunctions of a Team: A Leadership Fable*. San Francisco, CA: Jossey-Bass.

[4] Brown, B. (2018). *Dare to Lead: Brave Work. Tough Conversations. Whole Hearts*. New York: Random House.

[5] Keller, S., & Price, C. (2011). *Beyond Performance: How Great Organizations Build Ultimate Competitive Advantage*. Hoboken, NJ: Wiley.

[6] Gawande, A. (2010). *The Checklist Manifesto: How to Get Things Right*. New York: Picador.

[7] Salas, E., Tannenbaum, S.I., Kraiger, K., & Smith-Jentsch, K.A. (2012). The science of training and development in organizations: What matters in practice. *Psychological Science in the Public Interest*, 13(2), 74–101.

[8] Duhigg, C. (2012). *The Power of Habit: Why We Do What We Do in Life and Business*. New York: Random House.

[9] Fowler, S. (2016). *Why Motivating People Doesn't Work... and What Does: The New Science of Leading, Energizing, and Engaging*. Oakland, CA: Berrett-Koehler Publishers.

[10] Argyris, C. (1991). Teaching smart people how to learn. *Harvard Business Review*, 69(3), 99–109.

[11] Weick, K.E., & Sutcliffe, K.M. (2007). *Managing the Unexpected: Resilient Performance in an Age of Uncertainty*. San Francisco, CA: Jossey-Bass.

[12] Boyatzis, R.E., & McKee, A. (2005). *Resonant Leadership: Renewing Yourself and Connecting with Others Through Mindfulness, Hope, and Compassion*. Boston, MA: Harvard Business School Press.

[13] Goleman, D. (1995). *Emotional Intelligence: Why It Can Matter More Than IQ*. New York: Bantam Books.

[14] Paul, R., & Elder, L. (2006). *The Thinker's Guide to the Socratic Method*. Dillon Beach, CA: Foundation for Critical Thinking.

[15] Rogers, C.R. (1961). *On Becoming a Person: A Therapist's View of Psychotherapy*. Boston, MA: Houghton Mifflin.

[16] Kluger, A.N., & DeNisi, A. (1996). The effects of feedback interventions on performance: A historical review, a meta-analysis, and a preliminary Feedback Intervention Theory. *Psychological Bulletin*, 119(2), 254–284.

[17] Schön, D.A. (1983). *The Reflective Practitioner: How Professionals Think in Action*. New York: Basic Books.

[18] Stone, D., Patton, B., & Heen, S. (2010). *Difficult Conversations: How to Discuss What Matters Most*. New York: Penguin Books.

[19] London, M. (2003). *Job Feedback: Giving, Seeking, and Using Feedback for Performance Improvement*. Mahwah, NJ: Lawrence Erlbaum Associates.

[20] Loehr, J., & Schwartz, T. (2003). *The Power of Full Engagement: Managing Energy, Not Time, Is the Key to High Performance and Personal Renewal*. New York: Free Press.

[21] Heath, C., & Heath, D. (2010). *Switch: How to Change Things When Change Is Hard*. New York: Broadway Books.

Looking Ahead

The Language of Empowerment is the first title in ***The Language Series of Business Books***—a growing collection of practical guides designed to help leaders work with clarity, rhythm, and belief—where it matters most.

Each book in the series explores a different facet of leadership, organisational growth, and behavioural change, always grounded in tools that work in the real world—not just the classroom.

Here's what's already here—and what's coming next:

Book 2: The Language of Adaptation – Leadership System Design

Change doesn't fail because people resist—it fails because systems drift.
This second book offers a grounded, practical guide to leading through change by building systems that are clear, repeatable, and resilient. It's written for leaders at all levels who are ready to move from managing reactions to designing what good looks like—and sustaining it.

Book 3: The Language of Habits – Live Your Best Life (For Real This Time)

Not every setup sets you up.
This book is for young adults—and those guiding them—who never got the manual for how to live with rhythm, clarity, and purpose. Grounded in behavioural science and systems thinking, it reimagines life design as a habit-based flow, helping readers build the foundational routines that make adulthood work.

Also in development :

The Language of Quality – Assessing Operational Excellence
The Language of Identity – Transforming Organisational Culture

Each title in the series continues the same core promise:
To turn deep insight into practical language.
To make leadership habits visible, transferable, and sustainable.
And to equip you—no matter your title—to build what lasts.

The work continues.
So does the conversation.

www.ingramcontent.com/pod-product-compliance
Lightning Source LLC
Chambersburg PA
CBHW032039290426
44110CB00012B/865